Access Learning Zone.com

Microsoft Access 2010
Beginner Level 1

Course Handbook Supplement

By Richard Rost

Published By
Amicron Computing
www.AccessLearningZone.com

© Copyright 2012 by Amicron Computing
All Rights Reserved

Welcome

Welcome to **Microsoft Access 2010 Beginner Level 1.**

This handbook is designed to be a **supplement** to the full 599CD video course for **Microsoft Access 2010 Beginner Level 1**. We recommend you use this handbook to follow along with the class videos. This handbook is not meant as a stand-alone study guide.

We do recommend that you watch the course videos one time through, paying attention to the lessons covered. Follow along with the course videos using this guide. Take notes on the pages where needed. Then, watch the videos a second time, practicing the examples yourself on your own database.

Video Tutorials

Along with the purchase of this handbook, you are allowed free online access to the video tutorials. You can find them at this address: `http://599CD.com/XACB1PDF`

Table of Contents

Introduction	3
Lesson 1: Terminology	6
Lesson 2: Planning Your Database	12
Lesson 3: The Access Interface	17
Lesson 4: Customer Table	25
Lesson 5: Customer Tables Part 2	32
Lesson 6: Customer Table	37
Lesson 7: Entering Data	40
Lesson 8: Sorting & Filtering	45
Lesson 9: Queries	52
Lesson 10: Forms	64
Lesson 11: Customer Reports	76
Review	93

Introduction

Welcome to **Microsoft Access 2010 Beginner Level 1** brought to you by AccessLearningZone.com.
I am your instructor Richard Rost.

This class is for the **Beginner** with little experience building Microsoft Access databases. This is the introductory course in our Access series and is designed to teach you the absolute basics of how to build a database. If you've never used Access before then you're in the right place, start with this course, however even if you've been working with Access for some time you will still benefit from taking this class even **Expert** or **Advanced** users will still pick up a few tips and tricks from these lessons.

Our goal for today is to get you up and running as quickly as possible building your first Microsoft Access database.

- Database Terminology
- **Planning Your Database**
- The Access Interface
- Building a Customer Table
- Entering & Editing Data
- Sorting & Filtering
- Customer Queries
- Constructing a Customer Form
- Customer Reports & Labels

We will begin by learning some terminology, the benefits of using a database, and will discover the various components. You will learn how to properly plan out your database and determine what different Tables, Queries, Forms and Reports you'll need. We will go over the Microsoft Access design interface including the new ribbon menu. You will learn how to build your very first Table to track customers. You will learn about the different types of data that you can store, Table Fields and about Primary Keys. You will learn how to fill in and edit that data and how to work with records.

We will see how to sort and filter our data. Then you'll learn how to build a couple of different Queries to display information in different ways. You'll construct a Form to provide a nice user-friendly interface for working with data on the screen and you'll learn how to generate printable Reports including a Customer list and mailing labels. This course is designed to be used to Microsoft Access 2010, if you are using Access 2007 you shouldn't have any problems following along as the two versions are very similar.

If you're using Access 2003 or earlier you should either upgrade your version of Access or visit my website at AccessLearningZone.com and look for my Access 2003 tutorials. Access 2003 is radically different from 2007 and 2010. As mentioned earlier this is the introductory course for Microsoft Access but you should already have a basic working knowledge of Microsoft Windows before starting these lessons. You should know how to use the keyboard and mouse, start programs, maximize and minimize Windows, scroll bars and understand the difference between the backspace and delete keys. If any of these concepts seem unfamiliar to you, then you should go to AccessLearningZone.com and look for my Windows Beginner tutorials.

Windows Basics
- Knowledge of Windows
- Use the Keyboard & Mouse
- Start Programs
- Maximize & Minimize Windows
- Use Scroll Bars
- Backspace & Delete Keys

Optionally it is helpful but not required to know how to use Microsoft Word and/or Excel before learning Access. Many of the basic concepts taught in Word and Excel will help you understand Access better. A basic familiarity with the ribbon, editing and formatting text using the clipboard and working with rows and columns in a spreadsheet will help you when it comes to learning Access. If you're going learn how to use all three programs I recommend you learn them in the order of Word first then Excel second and then finally Access. Word-processing and spreadsheets are easier to learn, so if you have a choice start with those first then move up to Access. I have tutorials for Word and Excel, they also available on my website WordLearningZone.com and ExcelLearningZone.com.

My courses are broken up into four groups **Beginner**, **Expert**, **Advanced** and **Developer**. My **Beginner** courses are for novice users with little or no experience of Microsoft Access, they are designed to give you an overview of the basic features of Access and cover just what you need to know to be productive. The **Expert** series is designed for more experienced users who are already comfortable with Access. **Expert** classes go into a lot more depth about each topic then **Beginner** classes do and will cover more functions, features, tips and techniques for power users. When you've mastered the **Expert** classes move up to the **Advanced** lessons. You will learn how to work with macros, automation and many more advanced features that really enhance and add professionalism to your databases. Finally my **Developer** level courses are designed to teach you how program in Visual Basic for Microsoft Access, this will allow you to create the most advanced databases possible and unlock the full potential of Microsoft Access.

Each of my series are broken down into different numbered levels, starting with Level 1. Each subsequent level teaches you new and different topics in Microsoft Access building on the lessons learned in the previous classes. When you've finished all the **Beginner** classes move up to the **Expert** series, then the **Advanced** and finally **Developer** lessons, In addition to my normal Access classes I also have special **Seminars** designed to teach specific topics. Some of my seminars include building Web-Based Databases, creating Forms and Reports that look like Calendars, Securing your database, working with Images and attachments, writing Work Orders, Tracking Accounts Payable, Learning the SQL programming language and lots more. You can find details on all the **Seminars** and more on my website AccessLearningZone.com.

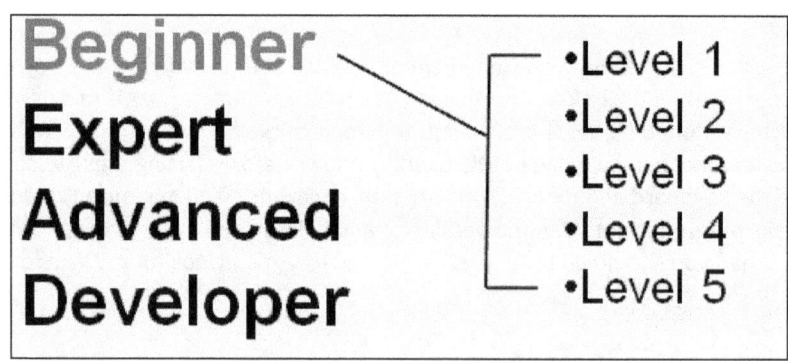

If you have questions about the topics covered in today's lessons please feel free to post them in our Interactive Student Forums. If you're watching this course using our custom video player software or online in the web theater you should see the student forum for each lesson appear in a small window next to the class video as long as you have an active Internet connection. Here you will see all of the questions that other students have asked as well as my responses to them and comments that other students have made. I encourage you to read through these questions and answers as you start each lesson and feel free to post your own questions and comments as well. If you're not watching your lessons online you can still visit the student forum later by going to AccessLearningZone.com/forums. Here you can also subscribe to the forum updates and receive a notification anytime anyone posts a question or comment.

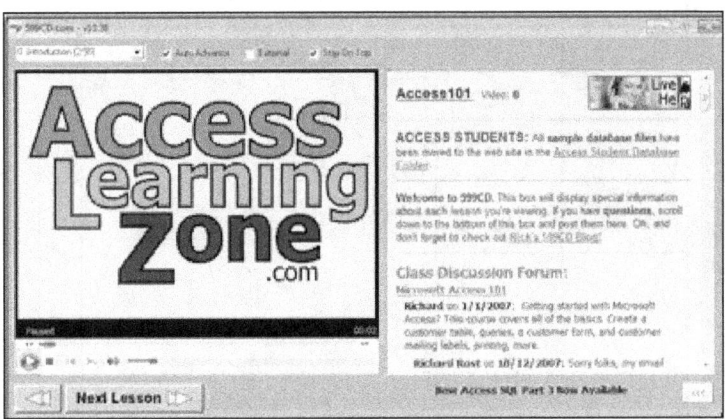

To get the most out of this course I recommend you sit back relax and watch each lesson completely through once without trying to do anything on your computer then replay the lesson from the beginning and follow along with my examples. Actually create the same database that I make in the video step-by-step. Don't try to apply which you're learning right now to other projects until you've mastered the sample database from this class. If you get stuck or don't understand something watch the video again from the beginning or tell me what's wrong in the student forum. I'll do my best to try and help. Most importantly keep an open mind, Access might seem intimidating at first but once you get the hang of it you'll see that it's really easy to use. While I encourage you to actually build the database that I build in today's class if you would like to download a sample copy of my database file you can find it at AccessLearningZone.com/databases.

Now let's take a closer look at exactly were going to learn in today's class.
In Lesson 1 we're going learn about Database Terminology. You'll learn what a Database is and you'll learn about the parts of an Access Database including Tables, Queries, Forms and Reports.
In Lesson 2 we'll discuss planning your Database, what Tables you'll need, what Fields should go in each Table, what do you want your Forms and Reports to look like.
In Lesson 3 we're going learn about the Microsoft Access Interface.
In Lesson 4 we're going to begin building our Customer Table.
In Lesson 5 we're continuing to build the Customer Table.
In Lesson 6 we will begin entering data into our Customer Table.
In Lesson 7 we're continuing to enter data into our Customer Table.
In Lesson 8 we're going to learn how to Filter and Sort the data in our Tables.
In Lesson 9 we will learn how to build a Query, apply a multi-field Sort to the Query and a Criteria Filter.
In Lesson 10 we're going to build a Customer Form so we can present our user with a nice friendly interface for editing records.
In Lesson 11 we will build a couple of different Customer Reports including some Customer Mailing Labels.

Lesson 1: Terminology

In Lesson 1 we're going learn about database Terminology. You'll learn what a database is and you'll learn about the parts of an Access database including Tables, Queries, Forms and Reports.

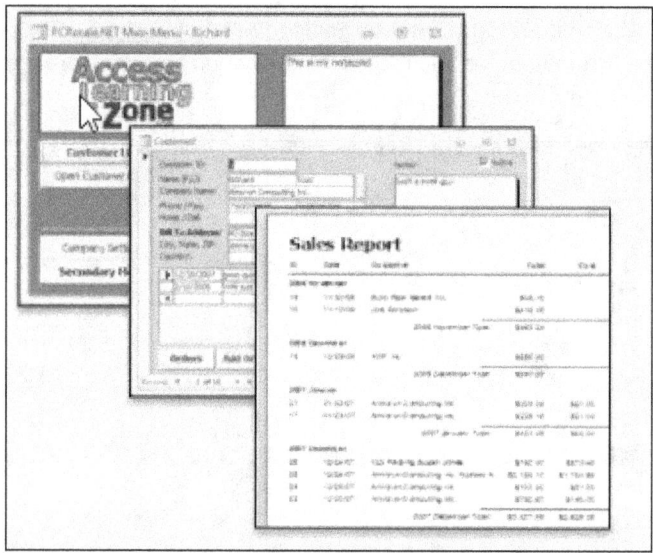

Before we get working with Access today lets go over some basic database terminology. A computer database is a program that lets you store, organize and manipulate data. Databases are great for storing large amounts of information, you can use a database to organize that information that is generated in different Reports and Queries and you can use a database to manipulate the data and make changes to it.

In the days before computers data would be stored on paper, usually in a ledger book on index cards, for example, to keep track of your customers you can make a series of index cards with one customer per card. You would have a separate drawer of cards for the products you sold or the suppliers you did business with. However as efficient as this may have seemed at the time it was very time-consuming to sort the cards or to search through a large drawer of cards for some the data.

When computers first came along the earliest databases were really nothing more than glorified text documents. They were great at storing information and they certainly made searching and sorting data easier, however they lack many features we take for granted for today, such as the ability to recognize relationships between different types of data, for example you could have your list of customers with some basic details, but if you want to look up information on those Customer's purchases you would have to look at another file. The earliest databases had no way to relate this information together. This creates many problems including having multiple copies of the same information in different places. Updating all that information can be a nightmare. Fortunately Microsoft Access does recognize Relationships and that's one of its strong points but much more on that later.

The next logical progression was to for people to store all of their data in an Excel spreadsheets. Now Excel is a great tool for storing small amount of information and for analyzing data but when it comes to large amounts of information using Excel can be cumbersome. If you've got more than a few thousand rows of data you really should be using a database program like Microsoft Access. Plus Excel has the same problem that early databases did, it's not relational, there's no easy way to link your Customers to their orders or products to their suppliers and so on.

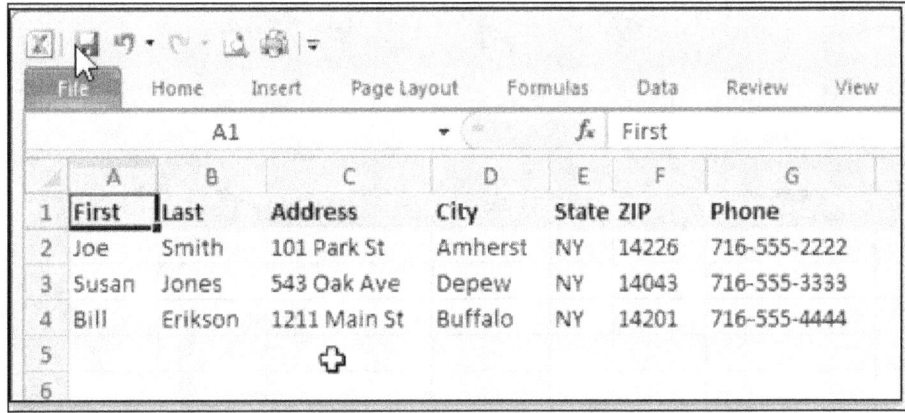

In addition Excel can be difficult for novice users to work with, if you don't know how to use Excel, finding the information that you want can sometimes be daunting. Whereas with Access you can build a nice user-friendly interface for beginners to easily find their way around in. Plus it's much easier to secure an Access database then Excel spreadsheet. You can control exactly what users can do in your database and what information they have access to.

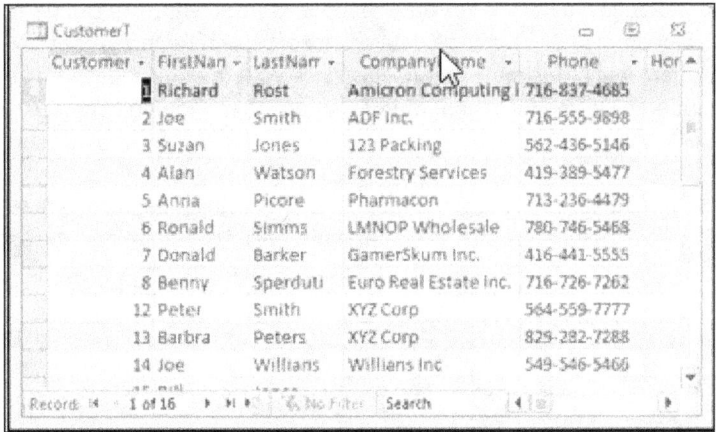

This brings us finally to the modern database. In my opinion Microsoft Access is the best desktop database application available. An Access database can store large amounts of data, much more than an Excel spreadsheet or a simple text document. An Access database can recognize relationships between your data for example if you're keeping track of customers and their orders you can store all of your customer details in one place and all of their order information in another place. Access can then relate the two together so you don't need lots of redundant information in a database such as having to copy all of your customer details onto each order. The database can keep track of that for you automatically.

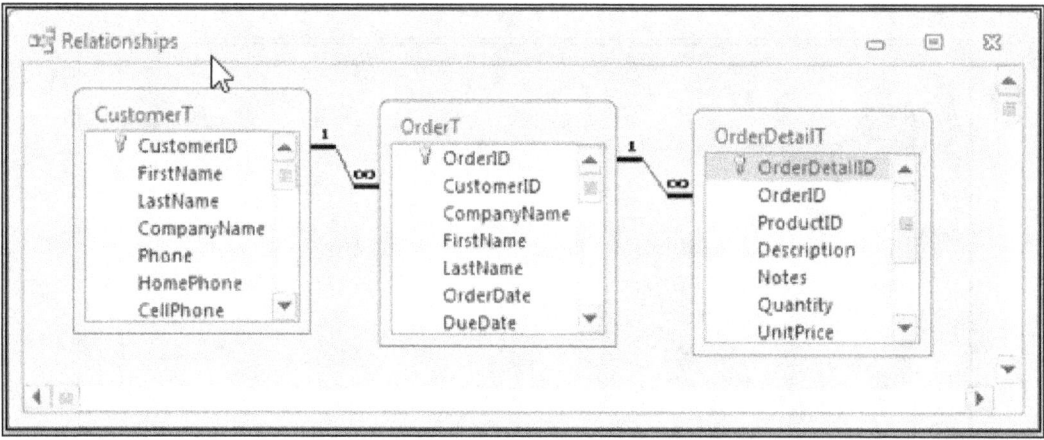

One of the problems with Excel spreadsheets and older database applications is that you have little or no control over what kinds of information gets put into your database. With Access you can specify exactly what the user can do. This will prevent for example a number where the customer's last name should be or a four digit phone number. Access gives you strict controls over the structure of your data and that's a great thing.

Access is great for you to build a database for other people to work with. You can design a very user-friendly interface so they don't get lost. All the data entry Forms and Reports that they need to work with can be presented for them in a nice simple menu. Plus since you, the developer, control the interface you can easily secure your database and lock them out of sections they shouldn't see. Sure it is a little bit of a learning curve to initially set your database up once it's built you will definitely save time.

Now that we know what a database is and what the benefits of using a database are let's talk about the parts of the Microsoft Access database. An Access database consists of data and the tools to work with that data.

Tables	Store data
Queries	Organize data
Forms	Display data on screen
Reports	Print out data
Macros	Automate tasks
Modules	Programming

What are these tools? An Access database consists of Tables, Queries, Forms, Reports and optionally Macros and Modules. Tables are used to store data, Queries to organize data, Forms to display on the screen, Reports to print out the data, and for advanced users you can build Macros to automate repetitive tasks and Modules which the full Visual Basic programming language inside inside your Access databases. Now I have macros and modules grayed out because you can build a fantastic database in Access without ever using them, all you really need our Tables, Queries, Forms and Reports.

All data in a Access database is stored in one or more Tables. You can think of a Table like a single Microsoft Excel spreadsheet however Tables give you much more control over the types of data that can be input into them. For example here you can see part of a Customer Table. Tables are made up of a collection of Fields, each Field holds a specific type of data. For example here I have highlighted the LastName Field in red:

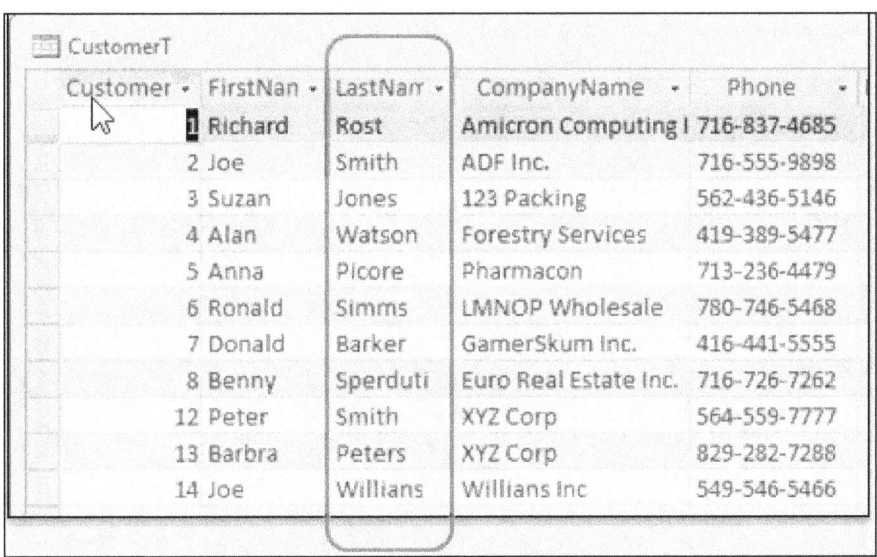

This Field should only store the Customer's last name and nothing else. In fact you can specify rules in the Table to force Fields to only contain certain types of information like text, numbers, dates or currency values.

Fields are also sometimes referred to as columns just like in an Excel spreadsheet. All of the data concerning one item is stored in a Record, each Record consists of every Field of data for that item. In this Customer Table for example each Record represents one Customer.
Here I have highlighted one Customer, Alan Watts, in red.

You can think of a Record like a row in an Excel spreadsheet. You might not always be storing customers however, in a product Table each Record would represent one product, in an order Table each Record would represent one order. In a timesheet Table for example each Record might represent one instance of an employee clocking in or out. So your Tables can store many different types of data, people, places, events and so on.

Now the data in your Tables might not be stored in any particular order. You might have hundreds of thousands of Records in your Table and the boss comes up even says "I only want a list of customers from New York sorted by last name" that's what a Query is used for.

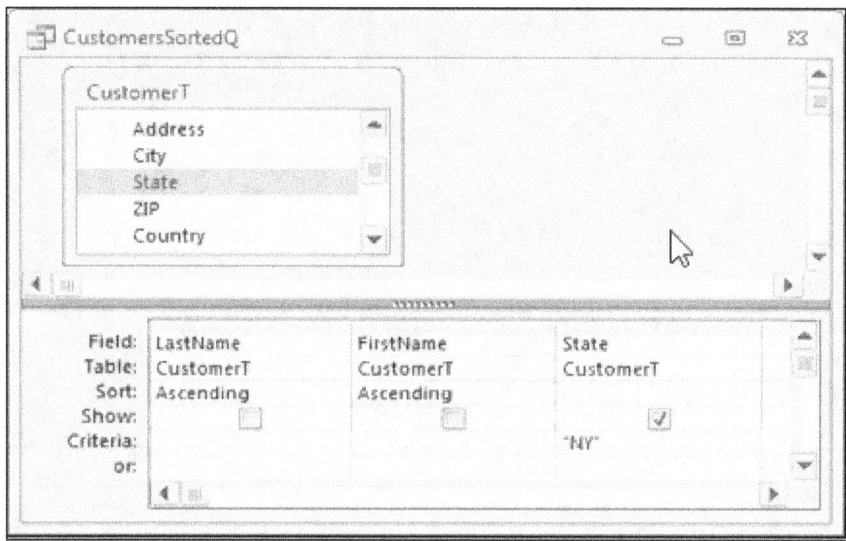

A Query is normally used to display data in different ways. You can Sort your data, or apply Criteria to only display certain types of data. Queries can be saved and used later so you don't have to keep redesigning them. Queries can also be used to modify data, add, delete or even used to modify records. We will learn more about those types of Queries in our **Expert** classes.

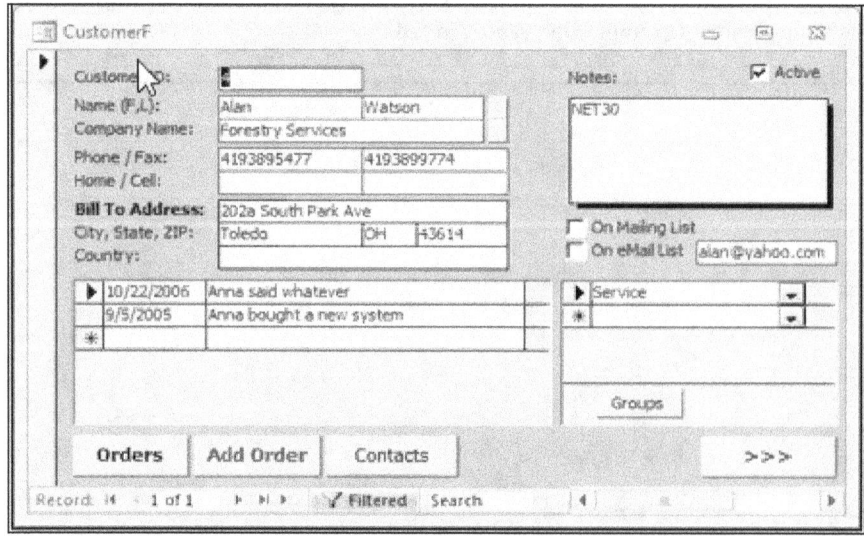

Forms allow you to build a nice user-friendly environment to work with your data on the screen. Whether you're building a database just for yourself or for other people to work with Forms are a major timesaver. You can display information however you want on a Form. You can include just the types of data that you want your users to work with. You can combine information from multiple Tables, such as displaying a summary of a customer's orders right on the customer screen. You can secure your fields so that users can only modify specific data. You can display calculations, on your Forms, such as the number of days an employee has missed work. Your Forms can also contain drop-down list so users can select from a list of data. Command buttons allow us to perform tasks such as opening other Forms; In fact you can turn a Form into a Main Menu for other Forms.

The benefits of working with Forms go on and on but essentially you'll build the interface with which your users will work with the database out of your Forms. You never want other users have to work directly with your Tables and Queries. You'll see why in upcoming classes.

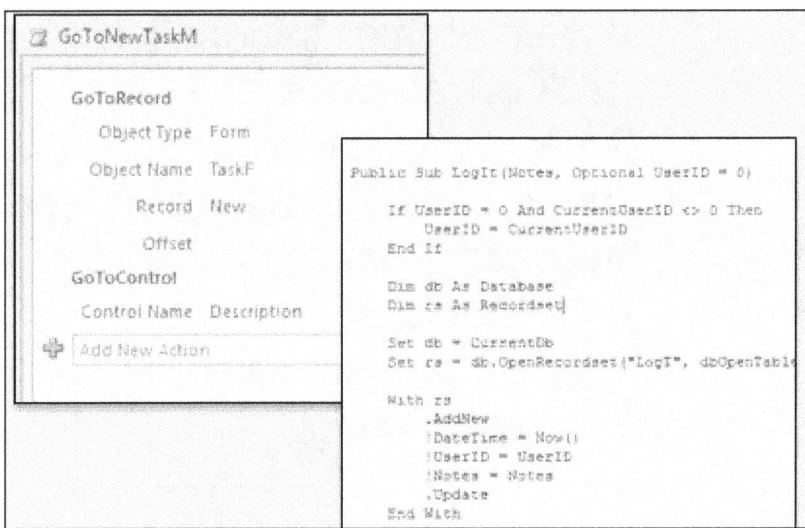

Reports are specifically designed to present data to people who are not using your database. You can print a Report out or send it to someone as an e-mail attachment. You could use reports for customer information, invoices, product catalogues, mailing labels, charts, a lot more. Anything you want to present to someone else can be presented in a Report.

Finally an Access database can contain Macros and Modules. These are more advanced topics we will cover in later classes. In a nutshell Macros are generally used to automate repetitive tasks or carry out simple actions. Modules contain Visual Basic programming code that can really take your database to a Professional level. Again you can build a great database without ever touching a macro or module and we'll cover these in our **Advanced** classes.

Lesson 2: Planning Your Database

This lesson we will discuss planning your database. What Tables do you need, what Fields should go in each Table, What do you want your forms and reports to look like?

Consider Your Needs

- Store customer information
- Track correspondence
- Generate mailing labels
- Create quotes & invoices
- Store order history
- Track employee timesheets
- Maintain product inventory
- Basic accounting

The first thing to do when planning a new database is to sit down with a piece of paper or a whiteboard and write down exactly what you want the database to do. Plan this out in advance, make a list of all the features that you want included in your database. What kinds of information do you want to store, customer information, be able track correspondence with those people, generate mailing labels to customers, create quotes and invoices, store each of your customer's order history, track employee time sheets, maintain a product inventory and perhaps even print out your product catalog straight from your database? Basic accounting, Accounts Receivable, Accounts Payable, whatever you want your database to do make a big list and write everything down.

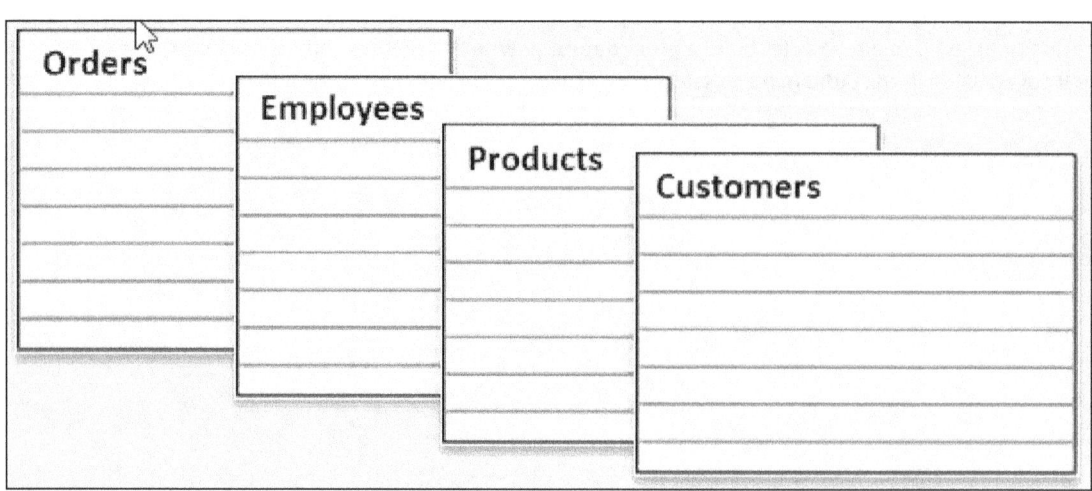

Now once you've decided all the things you want your database to be able to do sit down and determine what kinds of Tables you are going to need. Remember Tables store the data in your database. You want all of one kind of information in the same Table. So for example we're going to track information on our customers so we'll need a customers Table. Track information on products so I'm going to need a products Table. Products and customers are two totally unrelated things so each gets its own Table. Just like employees, employees get their own Table.

I'm also going to create an orders Table. Now orders may be related to products and customers because customers will purchase products and those will go into orders but the order information itself will go in its own Table. An order is its own kind of entity. Now we will talk a lot more about Relationships between Tables in future classes but for now I want you to put everything that stands on its own in its own Table.

Now that you've got an index card for all of the Tables that you want in your database, go through each Table and write down a list of the different types of Fields that you would like to have in each Table. Remember each specific item of information is considered a Field. If you're putting this into an Excel spreadsheet a Field would be a column of data. So for example I have basic information about my customer, first name, last name, address, city, state, zip code or postal code, phone number, and fax number. There's also some additional information I'd like to keep track of. For example is this customer on my mailing list? How long has he been a customer? Which I call customer since. What's this customer's credit limit? His e-mail address and any other extraneous notes I might want to keep track about this customer.

Customers	
FirstName	MailingList
LastName	CustomerSince
Address	CreditLimit
City	Email
State	Notes
PostalCode	
Phone	
Fax	

Make sure your as specific as possible when defining your fields. For example you don't want just one Field to track name and put first name and last name together in it, that's poor database design, it's very difficult later on if you want to pull some information out. For example if you want to Sort by last name and you've got first name and last name together in that Field it's very difficult to Sort just on last name. Or if you're writing letters and you want to say Dear Joe, you have frist and last name together so again it's very difficult to separate them. whereas it's easier to put stuff together should you have first name and last name separated you can easily put them together.

The same rule applies for address, don't just have address one and address two. You want Address, City, State, Postal Code. I've seen some databases that you separate the street number from the street name. You'll have 101 Main St separated. That level of complexity is completely up to you but you want to breakdown the information as much as possible, within reason.

Now you might notice when writing down my Field names I didn't put any spaces between first and name. Access databases work better if you don't use spaces in the Field names. I'll explain why in much more detail later on when we get to our **Advanced** classes but when you start writing VB code and Macros and SQL statements if you have Field names and Table names with spaces in them things start to get a little messy. So capitalize first and name but put them together without a space between. You'll see the same rule applies to mailing list, customer since, credit limit, and postal code.

Customers

FirstName	MailingList
LastName	CustomerSince
Address	CreditLimit
City	Email
State	Notes
PostalCode	OrderAmount1
Phone	OrderAmount2
Fax	OrderAmount3

You'll also notice that in my customer Table I do not have any fields to store information on the customer's orders. For example I've seen some people build databases where in their customer Table they'll have order one, order two, order three, that's bad database design, you want that information regarding the orders to be in a separate order Table. In the order Table you track the details for those orders, the order date, the sales rep, the order total, and sales tax collected, whether or not it was delivered and so on. This information gets stored in a separate table because now there's no limit to the number of orders that each customer can have. They may have no orders, they could have fifty orders, whereas before if you set the order Fields inside the customer Table you're limiting the number of orders for each customer.

Orders

OrderDate
SalesRep
OrderTotal
SalesTax
Delivered

Now if this seems a little confusing don't worry about it. We're going to spend a lot more time working with multiple tables and relationships between them once we get were **Expert** series. For today's class we're just going to focus on the customer Table but I want you to be aware that you should store different types of data in separate Tables.

The next step is to get some paper and draw out the way your Forms should look when your database is finished. Now as you can see I'm no artist but I do sit down and sketch out what I want each Form to look roughly on paper before I start building. Do you want a Main Menu with some different buttons? Click on this button to open up the customer Form, click on this button to open up the order Form and so on.

Then sketch out each of those forms. My customer info should have the details about a customer up top, first name, last name and so on. I'd like the customer's contact history at the bottom of the Form. Every time I talk to that customer I will put some notes in about we talked about, maybe a picture of the customer if it's available.

Just take a few minutes and sketch out what you want the database to look like. Remember keep in mind the skill level of the average user of your database. If you're building this database for other people to work with you want to make it as simple and as user-friendly for them. Plus having your Forms drawn-out acts like a roadmap, you can see on paper what you should be designing on the screen and it just makes it easier.

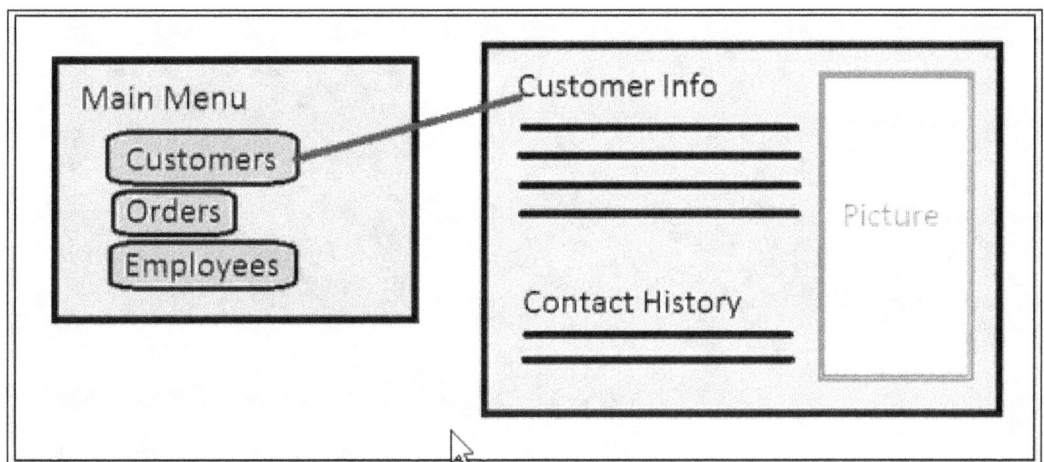

The next step, gather together all your printed Reports. You probably have paper Forms you are using now, or at least Reports you been generating with Excel or Microsoft Word. Get those altogether so you can see the different types of Reports that you're going to need to generate from your database. For example I've got an Accounts Receivable Report, an Invoice and some Mailing Labels.

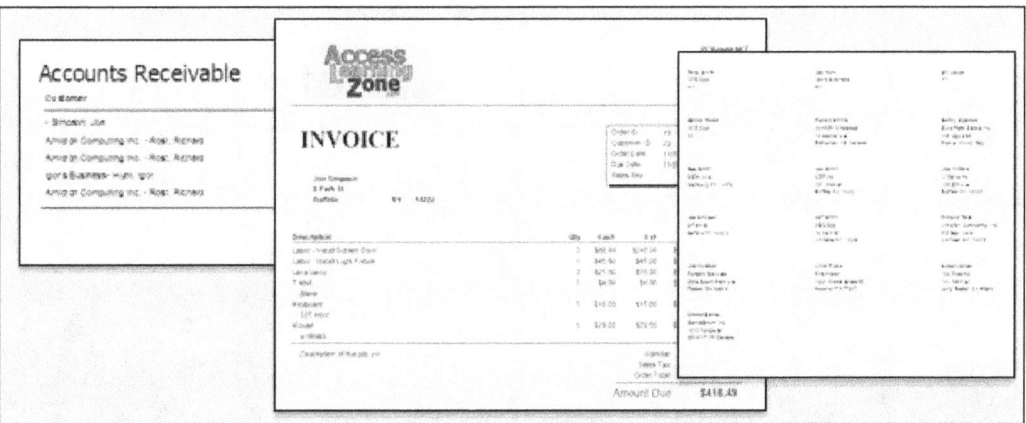

Make a list of all the different types of Reports that you expect your database to generate. The bottom line here is Plan Ahead! A complex database takes a lot of planning. You don't want to start building your database and then realize later on that you made a simple mistake that would have been caught had you planned everything out in the beginning. The more planning you do ahead of time the easier the job will be later when you're actually building your database. Now don't worry about laying out your Queries at this point, Queries are usually something you design on-the-fly, but do take the time to make yourself a list of Tables, the Fields needed in each one of those Tables, a rough sketch of what Forms you want and how you want your on-screen display to look, and what Reports the database should generate.

Lesson 3: The Access Interface

In Lesson 3 we're going learn about the different parts of the Microsoft Access Interface.

Let's begin by starting Microsoft Access. Now you might have a Quick Launch icon for Microsoft Access on your Windows task bar, like I do, or you might have a Desktop Shortcut for Microsoft Access 2010, but if not just take your mouse and click on the Start button in the bottom left corner. Now you might even see Microsoft Access show up on the Start Menu directly if you've used it recently but if not click on All Programs, click on the Microsoft Office folder and then click on Microsoft Access 2010.

This opens up Microsoft Access, now unlike Word and Excel, Access does not automatically start you in a blank document. We have to first create a database file. You'll see here, in the center of the window a section called available templates. Now Microsoft has provided you with some prebuilt databases that you can use if you're in a hurry.

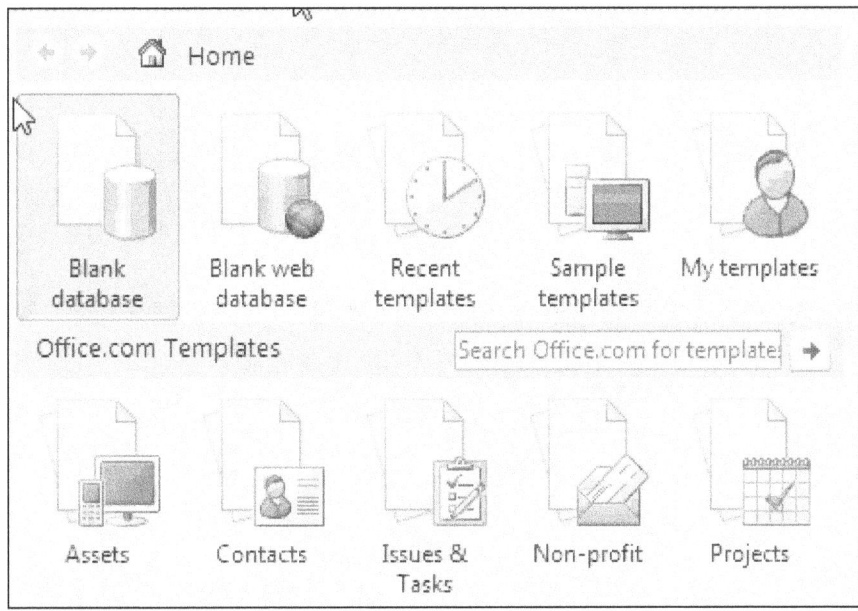

We're here today to learn how to build a database from scratch so I'm going to click on blank database. Now down in the bottom right corner you'll see a section to specify a filename for your database. Access wants to know what name you want to give your database. Right now it says *database1.accdb*. You may or may not see that **accdb** depending on your Windows settings and whether or not you see file extensions. In either case don't worry about it that just tells Windows that this is an Access database file.

You can leave the file named *Database1* if you want to but I like to give my databases descriptive names. So I'm going to click here and type in the *PCResaleCustomerDatabase*.

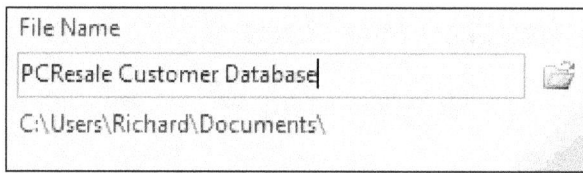

That is a fictional company that i've set up, call PCResale. We're going to build a customer database for this fictional company. Now below the filename you'll see the folder that Access is going to place this database file in. Right now mine is set in *C:\Users\Richard\Documents* and that's okay for me. If you want to change it you can click on the little folder button right here and browse for a different folder to place your database in, but since I'm happy with that folder I'm going to click on the create button.

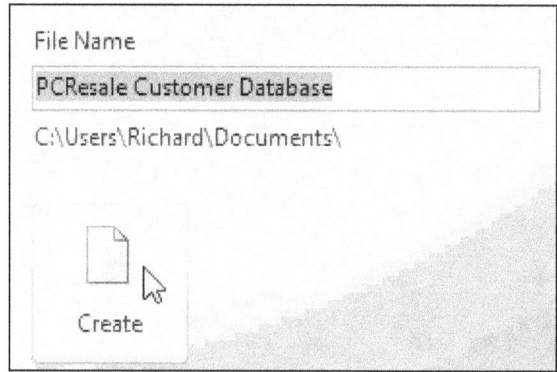

After you click on create, Access builds a blank database in the folder specified and wants to start building your first Table.

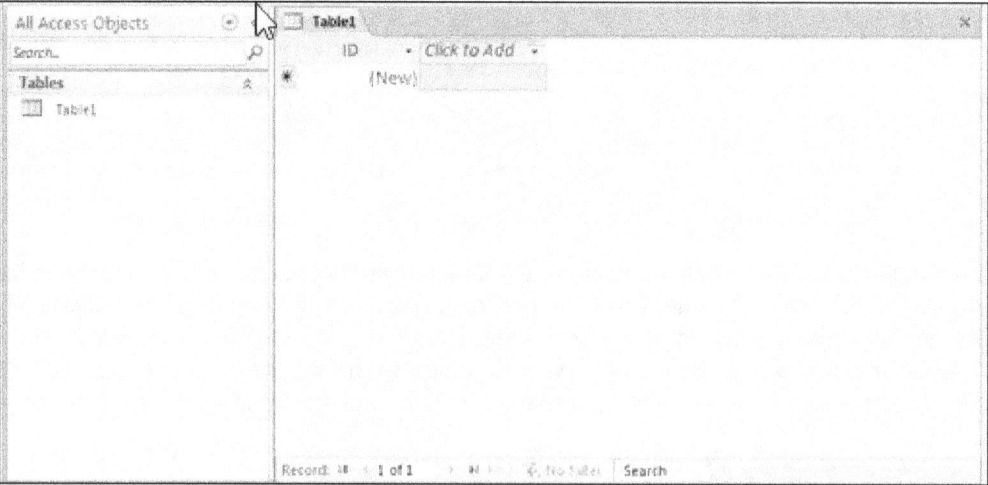

You'll see right here it says *Table1* and up top it says Table Tools.

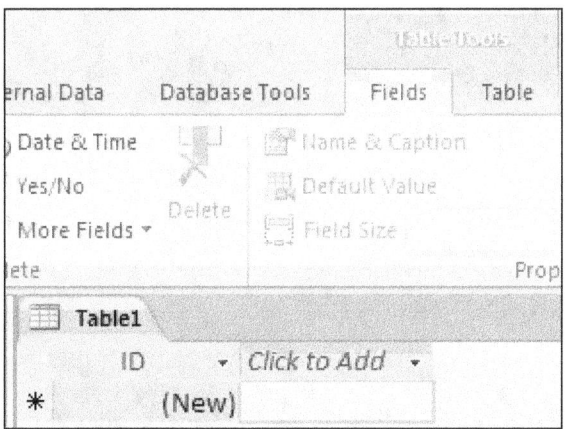

That's because Access started out by creating a blank Table for us, Now I don't want to start by just entering data into a blank Table. I want to define the Table first. I want to setup the rules for this Table so I'm going to come over here and click on this X that will close down this Table.

And now I'm left with a blank database container.

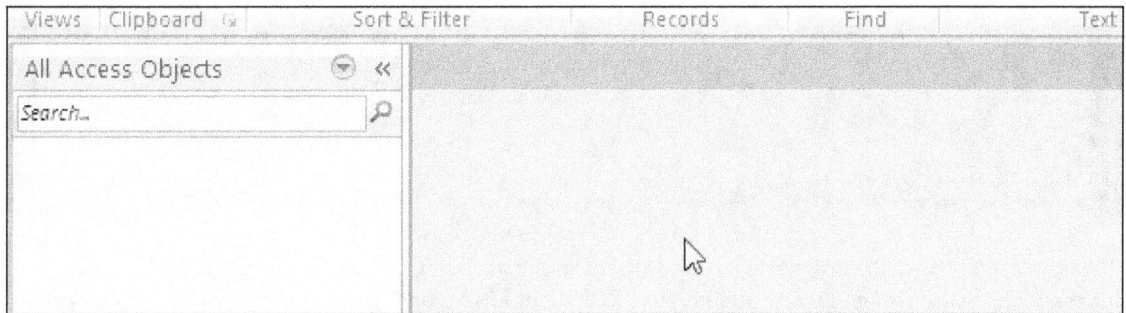

For a Microsoft Access database, all objects in the database, all the Tables and Queries and Forms and Reports and all the things we learned about earlier will be stored in one database file and that's the PCResale Customer Database that we just created. Right now its empty and we're going to put some stuff in it in a minute. Now before we start actually working with database lets learn about the parts of the Access interface.

If you've worked with Word or Excel you'll find a lot of this is the same, but there are a few different things. Across the very top of the Access window you'll find the *Title Bar*. The *Title Bar* will have the name of the current database, the file format that you're using, Now this says Access 2007, don't worry Access 2010 uses the Access 2007 file format, so that's perfectly normal and then ofcourse over here it says Microsoft Access.

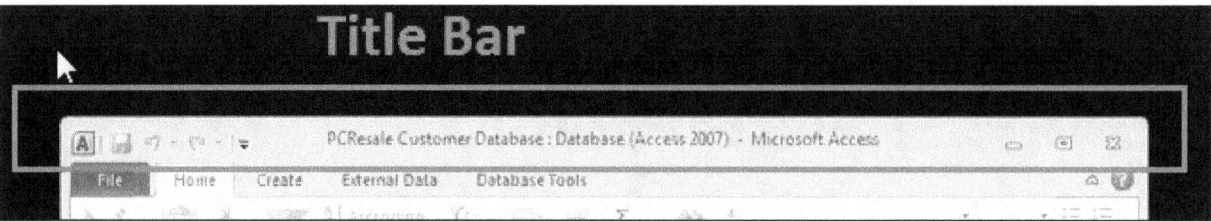

In the upper right corner we have are familiar window controls. These include the Minimize, Restore or Maximize buttons and the Close button below.

Below the *Title Bar* we have the *Ribbon*. The *Ribbon* is a new menu interface that was introduced in Access 2007. If you've used versions of Access before 2007 you'll find the *Ribbon* is a radically different menu interface.

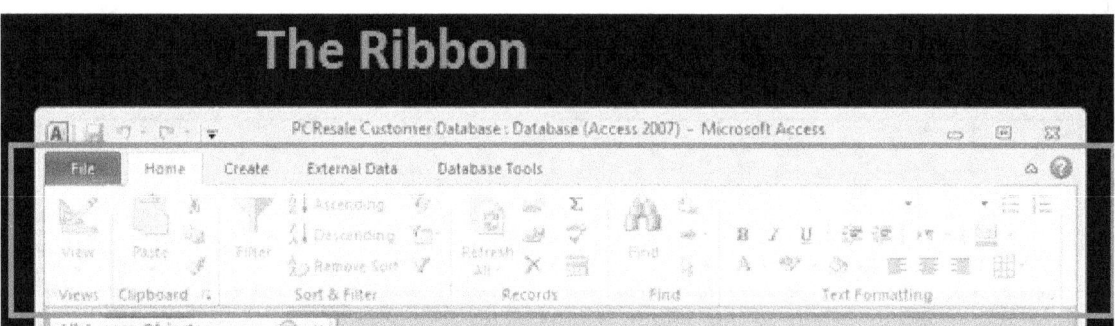

It was designed to group commands together to make things easier to find. Personally I didn't care much for the *Ribbon* when it first came out and Access 2007 but after working with it for a while I finally came around. The *Ribbon* really is better than the old menu interface. The *Ribbon* is divided up into different tabs. Here you can see the *Home* Tab. There is a File Tab, a *Create* tab where we will go to create objects, *External Data* for working with data outside of our database and more advanced *Database Tools*. We'll spend most of our time on the *Create* and *Home* tabs.

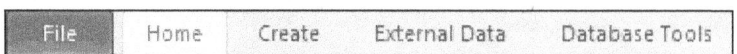

Now right now you'll see that most of the features on the *Home* tab are grayed out. That's because we don't have any objects in our database yet. We dont have any Queries, Tables or Forms to work with so we have to create those things on the *Create* tab.

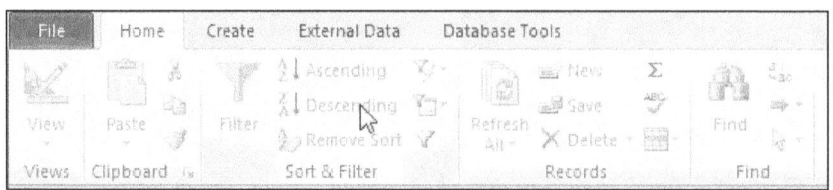

Inside each tab you can see the various command buttons are organized into groups. For example these are all the buttons here that deal with creating different Tables. Here you can see Queries and Forms and so on.

Now the *Ribbon* is designed to be dynamic it will change based on what you're doing. It will also change based on how large your Access window is. You can see as a resize my window the buttons on the *Ribbon* change, the groups will collapse or expand based on how much space they have available, so the menus you see on my screen might not look exactly the same on your screen. If you maximize your window or make it larger by resizing it you'll see the buttons take more space.

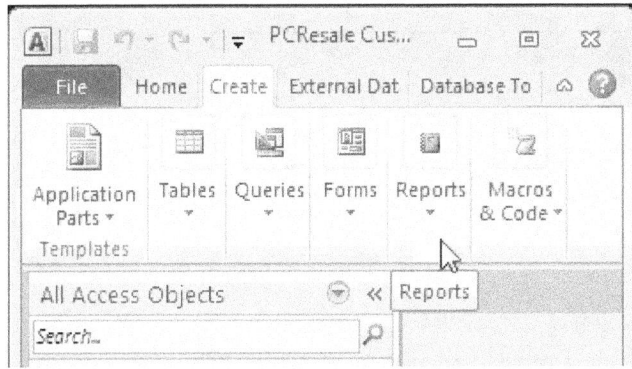 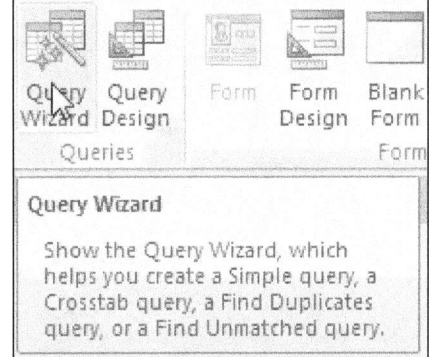

If you can't remember what a button does just hold your mouse over it and a pop-up menu appears and explains what that button's function is. Now there are a lot of buttons up here and we're not going to learn about all of them today but eventually we'll cover all the buttons you need to build a great database.

If screen space is at a premium and you don't have a lot of room in your window you can minimize the *Ribbon* by simply double-clicking on one of the *Ribbon* tabs. That will shrink it up and save you some more space. To bring it back just double click again and it will re-expand the ribbon.

You might see additional tabs on the *Ribbon* based on what you're doing. for example we started out earlier with a Table already open. If I click on *Create* and then Table you'll see the *Table Tools* section appears and there's two new tabs, *Fields* and *Table*. These are menu options that only appear if you're working with Tables. So as you can see Access automatically hides these commands if your not working with Tables, you don't need to see them.

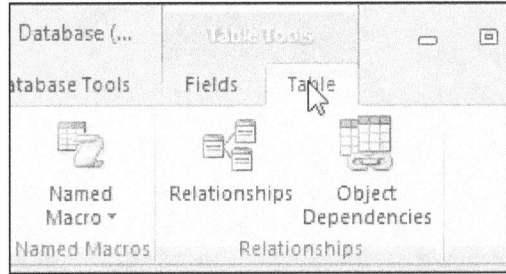

In the upper left corner of the window you'll find a Quick Access toolbar. The Quick Acess toolbar is right here and out-of-the-box Access comes with 💾 Save, ↶ Undo, and ↷ Redo as commands on this toolbar. We'll talk about what these commands do in a little bit but you can use the Quick Access toolbar to add commands that you use all the time, let's say for example that you always use the Table design, well you can right-click on it and go add the Quick Access toolbar and that will put a copy of that button right up here.

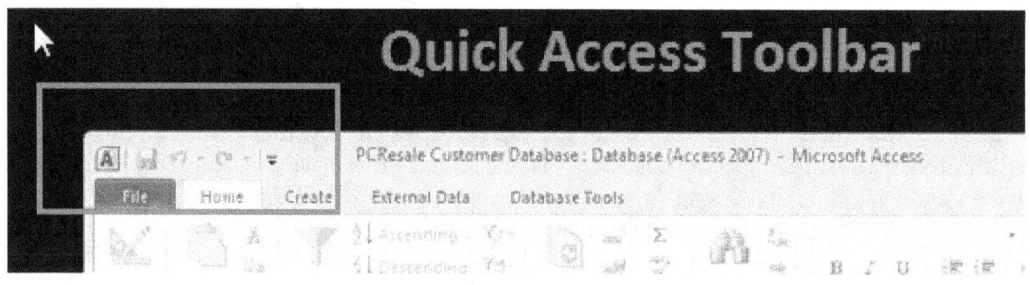

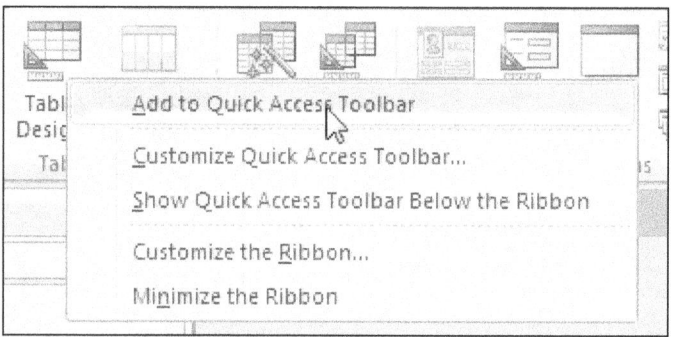

Now you have access to that button no matter where you are in the *Ribbon*. I'm going to get rid of it though by right clicking on it and selecting remove from Quick Access toolbar.

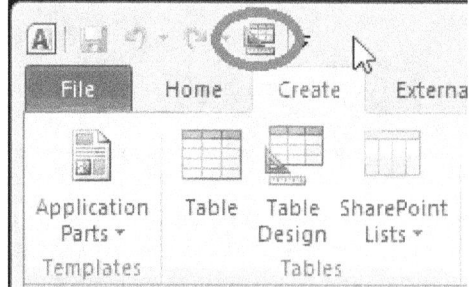

On the left side of the screen you'll find the *Navigation Pane*. This is where a list of all of your Access objects will appear, your Forms, Reports, Tables, Queries, and so on.

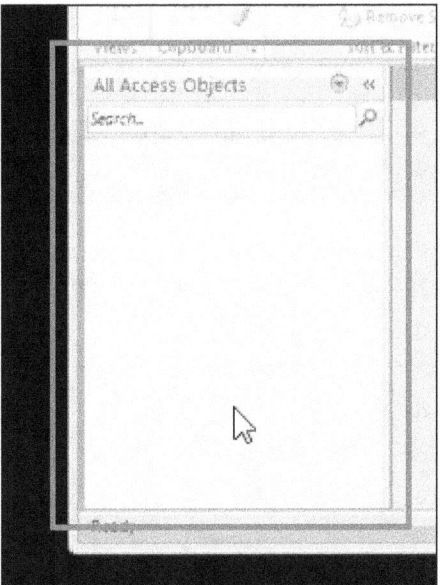

Here I've opened one of my other databases and you can see in the *Navigation Pane* a list of Tables. If I scroll down you'll see different groups for Queries, Forms, and Reports. I can open up these groups by clicking on the little double Chevron and that'll open up all the queries.

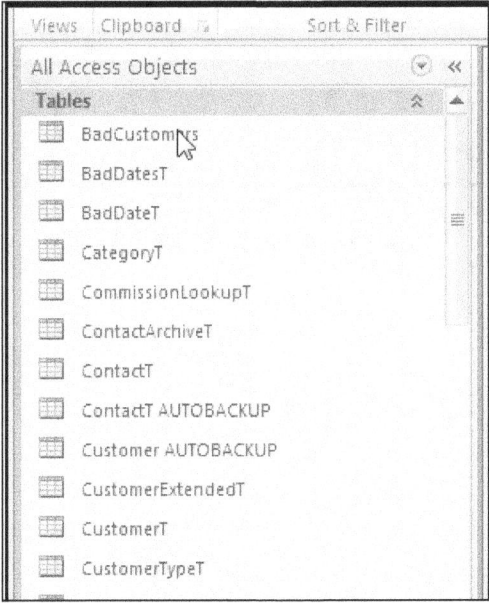 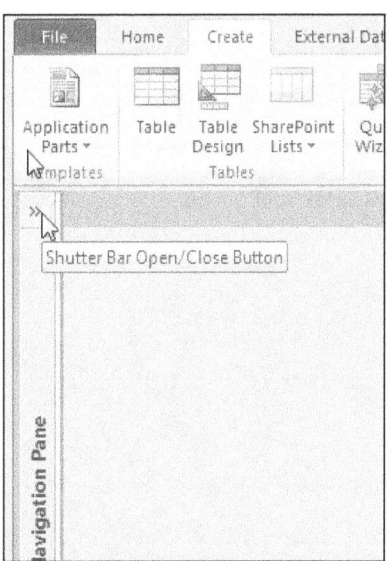

Until you create your first objects though your *Navigation Pane* will be blank. You can resize the *Navigation Pane* if you'd like to by clicking on its right most border and dragging. You can also hide it completely by clicking on «« this button right here and then »» this button again to open.

Way down near the bottom of the window you'll see the *Status Bar*. Most of the time the *Status Bar* just says "Ready" but it does pop up occasional messages. You can also program it with custom prompts, here for example it says "this is the customer's first name" when I click on the `FirstName` field in my customer Form. We'll see how to do this in the future lesson.

Access 2010 Beginner 1

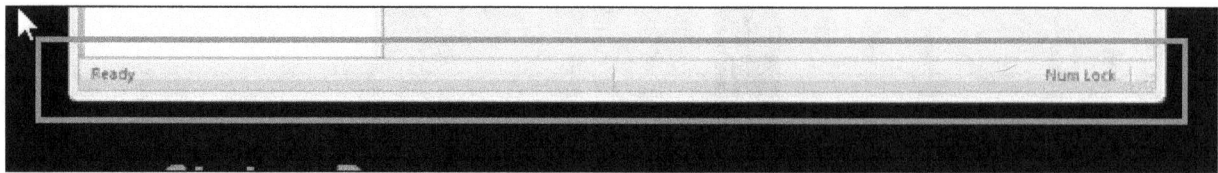

Finally we have this big area here call the *Object Pane*. This is where the objects in your database will appear when you open them up. You can see Tables, Queries, Forms, Reports, whatever other objects you open up.

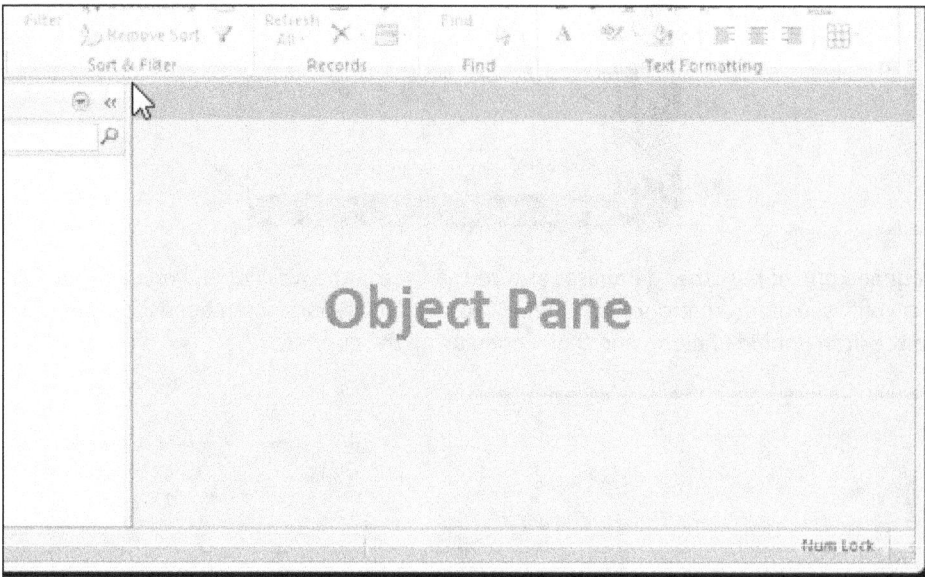

So that's a quick tour of the Microsoft Access interface, in the next lesson will begin by building our first Table.

Lesson 4: Customer Table

In Lesson 4 we're going to begin building our customer table.

Now we know way around the Access interface let's create our first Table. Go back to your index cards and find the one for your customer Table. These are all Fields going to add to the Table in the database.

```
Customers

FirstName      MailingList
LastName       CustomerSince
Address        CreditLimit
City           Email
State          Notes
PostalCode
Phone
Fax
```

Now there are two ways to create Table. Click on the *Create* tab and here you'll see Table and Table Design. Now Table by itself puts us in datasheet view and this is what Access started before. I personally don't like datasheet view, datasheet view is okay for entering data. But if you're designing a new Table I recommend using Design View.

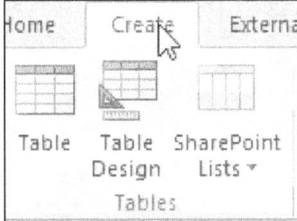

If you're going to create a new Table I recommend clicking on "*Create*" and then "*Table Design*". This is Table Design View. This is where we specify the structure of the Table first before putting any of the data in it and that's the main benefit of using a Table in Access is you can define the structure of the Table and enforce rules and what kinds of data go into each Field. Spreadsheet programs like Microsoft Excel just let anybody type anything anywhere on the sheet where with Access we want strict control over what information goes where.

Down below here you can see we have three columns. The first column is where we type in the Field name. Then we specify the data type what kind of information does the Field hold? Then optionally we can type a description. So let's start off with our first Field in this case `FirstName`.

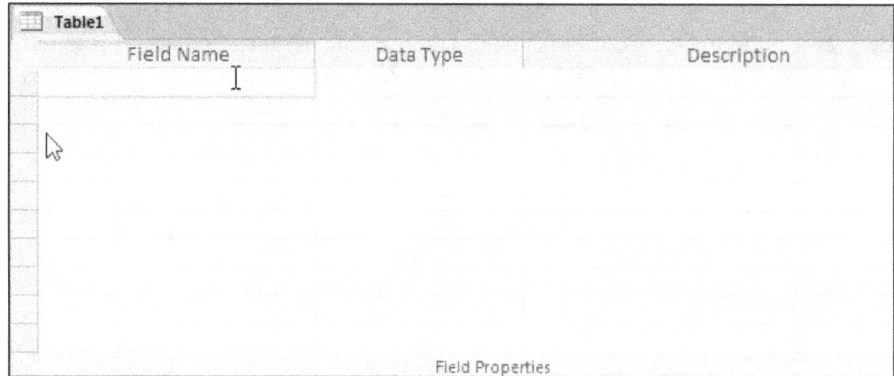

Remember I don't like putting spaces in my Field names. So its capital First no space capital Name. Now this is really more of a matter of style then anything else but this is my personal preferred style. You might see some other Access developers or authors of other books use underscores for example "first_name" that's perfectly fine too. In fact they might not even capitalize first name that's fine as well. The problem basically is that if you do use spaces in your Field names later on we get in the programming or writing Macros or some SQL statements you have to remember to put brackets around everything and that just becomes a pain.

So choose one method of naming your Fields and maintain consistency. Personally I recommend that you stick with my naming conventions. Once you've got `FirstName` typed then press the tab key. Now were at the data type column. This is where you specify what kind of data the `FirstName` Field is going to store. If you drop this box down you'll see the complete listing of all the different data types that Microsoft Access supports.

The first type of data is Text and you probably use text fields more than anything else. Text fields are most printable characters A-Z, a-z, 0-9 plus pretty much anything else in the keyboard that is a printable character. Text fields can be up to 255 characters long so they can store a decent amount of information.

Text

Most printable characters, A-Z, 0-9
Up to 255 characters long

The next datatype is a Memo fields. Memo fields are essentially very long Text fields. Where Text fields can only store 255 characters of data, a Memo field can store over 65,000 characters of data. Memo fields also support formated text. So if you want to bold or italicized text or maybe change the text color you can use a Memo field for that. Don't use Memo fields for everything though because they do lack some of the functionality that simple Text fields have. We'll talk about the differences in a future class. Essentially for small bits of information like someone's name or address or phone number use a text field. If you had to type in lots and lots of information or formatted text use a Memo field.

Memo

Very long text fields (65,000+ characters)
Support formatted text
Lack some functionality that text fields have

Next we have Numbers. Number fields can store either counting numbers also called Integers or Decimal values also called floating-point values. Unlike Text fields you can perform calculations on numbers so you can calculate the Sum or Average of a bunch of Number fields for example.

Numbers

Counting Numbers (Integers)
Decimals (Floating Point Values)

A Date/Time field can store either a Date or a Time or both. So you could have in January 1st 1980 or just 4:55 PM or you could have January 1, 1980 at 4:55 PM. Those are all valid Date/Time values.

Date/Time

January 1st, 1980
4:55 pm
January 1st, 1980 at 4:55 pm

Next have the Currency data type which is a special number that is optimized for dealing with dollar values ($).

Currency

Monetary Values

A Yes/No field stores either a True or False value. It may be called Yes/No, True/False, On/Off, these are called and Boolean values.

Yes/No

True/False
On/Off
Boolean Values

Next we have a very important datatype called an AutoNumber. An AutoNumber is essentially an automatic counter field. It will start at 1 with the first record and acts as automatic incerment that numbers for you with each following record so the next records 2 and 3 and so on. You don't need to worry about maintaining that AutoNumber yourself. We'll use AutoNumbers for identifying unique Records. Each customer will have had a `CustomerID` that is an AutoNumber.

```
AutoNumber

Automatic Counter
Starts at 1 and counts up
You don't need to worry about it
```

Next we have have OLE objects. OLE stands for Object Linking and Embedding and this is basically anything you can Copy and Paste in a window. It can be a picture, a document file, a video an Excel spreadsheet, a sound clip. Anything you can copy and paste in Windows can generally be stored in an OLE object.

```
OLE Object

Object Linking & Embedding
Pictures, Documents, Videos, etc.
Anything you can copy and paste
```

Similar to an OLE object, an Attachment data type field can store pretty much any kind of file in Windows. Attachment fields have some advantages and disadvantages, for example attachments can be compressed to save space in the database. We'll talk about the differences Attachments and OLE objects in a future lesson.

```
Attachment

Files you can store in your database
```

A Hyperlink field is good for storing a link to a webpage or an e-mail address. If the user clicks on the Hyperlink their web browser or e-mail program will launch automatically.

```
Hyperlink

Link to a Web page
Email address
```

A Calculated field stores the result of a calculation in your Table. For example you might have `SalePrice` minus `UnitCost` equals `Profit` and you can store that in a `Profit` field. Generally I dont recomend using calculated fields, we're going to do calculations in our Queries. There are some exceptions, we'll talk about those later.

Calculated

Stores result of a calculation
SalePrice – UnitCost = Profit

Finally we had to Lookup Wizard. The Lookup Wizard allows you to look up the value from another Table. For example you could use it to select a customer while you're in your order Table. Personally I don't like Lookup Wizards, we'll talk about Lookup Wizards in a future class.

Lookup Wizard

Looks up a value from another table
Select a customer in the order table

So now we know the basics of all the data types, which one do you think we should use for the `FirstName` field? That one's pretty easy, lets pick text for that one. Now you can optionaly type in a description over here. You don't have to, infact I will never use descriptions. You can type in this is the customer's first name and that will explain to someone else using the database what this field represents.

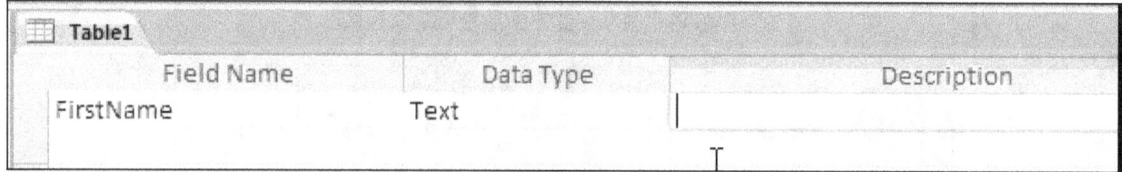

The description field will show up in the status bar on the bottom of form when a user is typing data into that field but again personally I almost never use them. So let's moved down here and type in the next field name. let's go with `LastName`, we'll also make that a text field.

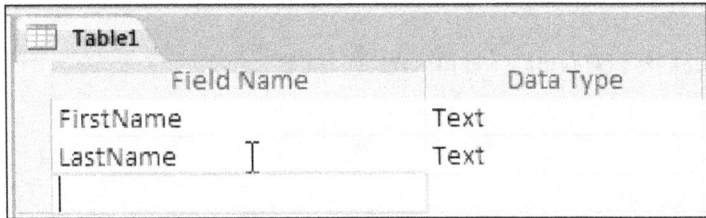

Now what about Fields for middle initial or middle name, prefix, like Mr. or Ms., suffix, like Snr or Jnr, that's completely up to you. Create as many Fields as you want to store whatever data you think you're ever going to need.

For the purposes of class I'm going to keep things simple and just use `FirstName` and `LastName`. That's all I ever use in my business. But again break down your information into as much as possible if you ever think you're going to need it in the future create a Field for it. It's much easier to put data fields together later on than it is to try and split them up. So if you ever think you're going to need a salutation Field add that in.

Continuing on I'm going to type in a `CompanyName` Field is also text. Let's add an `Address` field (that's also text.) Now I've always been happy with a single address field. Some people have `Address1`, `Address2`, I don't bother because an address line will wrap around with second line in and out on a Report. However I've also seen some people break the `Address` field down into the `StreetNumber`, the `StreetName`, and the `StreetType` whether it's a Drive, Avenue, and so on. So that's really a decision you have to make. For me personally I've always been happy with a single address line. I will create separate fields for `City`, `State`, `PostalCode` and `Country` and those are all text fields.

Lesson 5: Customer Tables Part 2

In Lesson 5 were continuing to build the customer Table.

What about some different types of data, well lets scroll down here, we can add pretty much as many Fields as we want to in the single Table. Yes there is an upper limit but you should realistically never hit it. Let's put in `Email` and let's make this a Hyperlink field, so when I click on the person's `Email` it will automatically launch my e-mail program.

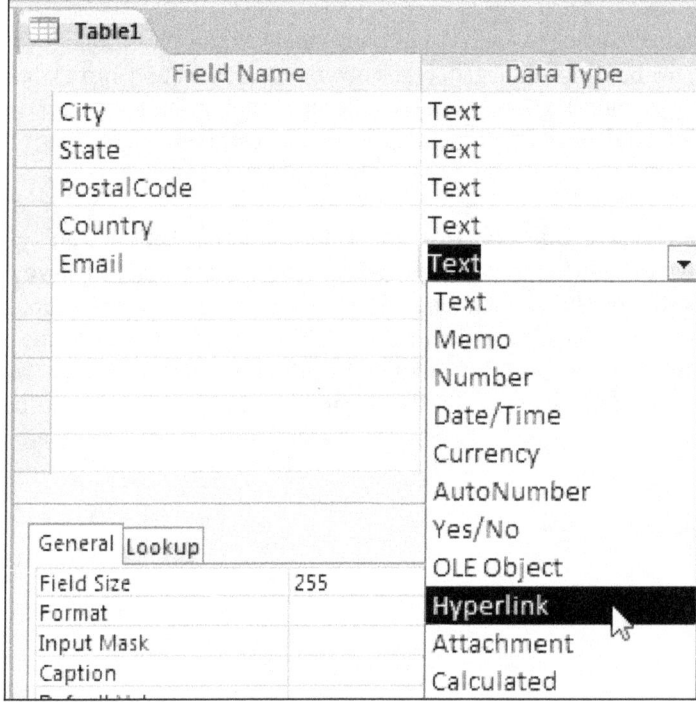

We can also type in `Website` and make that a Hyperlink as well. This time I'll just press H on my keyboard. Notice out automatically fills in Hyperlink.

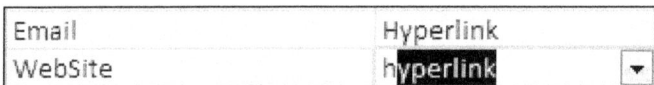

Next how about `PhoneNumber` or just `Phone`. Now this I'm going to also keep as text not a number. There are a couple of reasons why. First ask yourself are you ever going to be performing calculations on this data. Are you ever going to need to find the sum of a bunch of phone numbers or calculate their average? If so use a Number type if not use Text. Text handles these types of values better.

> **Calculations?**
>
> Need to find a sum or average? Use number. Otherwise, use text.

Another factor taken into consideration, leading zeros. Some Zip Codes start with a zero. Well if your using a Number field to store that, that zero will falloff and the value becomes 9832. So if the value you're going to store needs a leading zero stick with text.

Leading Zeros

ZIP codes like 09832
SSNs like 066-99-7654

Most obviously sometimes phone numbers can contain text. If you see a phone number somewhere for contact and it includes text values. You don't want to have to stop and grab your phone and translate those letters to numbers. You just type in the text right in your database.

Sometimes Contains Text

1-800-DRUIDIA

Another consideration usually comes in the play later is Sort Order. Numbers are always sorted numerically whereas Text values assorted alphanumerically. In an alphanumeric Sort for example 10 comes before 2.

Sort Order

Numbers: 1, 2, 3, 4, 10, 11, 12
Text: 1, 10, 11, 12, 2, 3, 4

So again knowing what we know now we'll stick with Text for a Number field. Next to keep track of how many employees a particular customer has, assuming the customer of course is a company, I'm going to type it in as `NumEmployees`. I'm going to abbreviate number with `Num`. That's okay, just maintain consistency. This is going to be a Number Field and need as I might sometime want to run a Report that says "show me a list of companies with more than 50 employees." I wouldn't be able to do that with a Text Field.

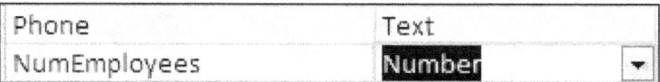

Now when it comes to Number Fields you can specify what kind of number you want. The default type is Long Integer. Long Integers are basically counting numbers 0123 and so on and their negatives. Sometimes however you might want a value that has a Decimal or Floating-point number. For example let's say we want to keep track of their discount rate. What type of discount does a customer get on his orders? Well that's going to be a Number and if we come down here in the field size, drop this box down you can see there are several different kinds of numbers that are available.

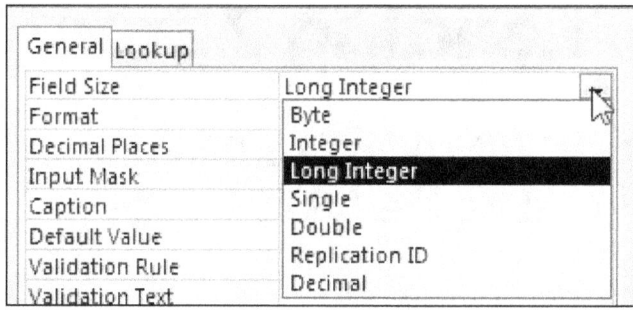

Now we're not going to talk about them all today, just be familiar with Long Integer for counting numbers and double if you need a decimal number. Now I'll pick double because I want a discount rate that might have a decimal point after 2.5% for example.

Next I would like to keep track of how long this customer's been with us so i can send loyalty cards. I like to send my customers been around for three years. For example so `CustomerSince` this will be a date time value. Let's keep track of each customer's `CreditLimit`. That will be a Currency value. We can program the database later to yell at us if there are outstanding orders are more than $5000 for example.

NumEmployees	Number
DiscountRate	Number
CustomerSince	Date/Time
CreditLimit	Currency

How about an "`IsActive`" field that will be a Yes or No value. Now this is where a Field might need some explanation. Someone who doesn't know your database might not know what is active means. You could put here in the description field on mailing list. And that will explain to an onlooker or someone using your database that if the customer is not marked active he won't receive my mailing list.

CreditLimit	Currency	
IsActive	Yes/No	On mailing list

Let's add in a `Notes` field that will be a Memo data type. I pretty much included a `Notes` field in just about every Table because almost everything that I can think of might need some extra notes attached to it. The benefit of `Notes` Field is that if you don't use them they don't take up any space in your database so it doesn't hurt to add a `Notes` field to each Table.

We still have no way to uniquely identify each Customer and that is what the AutoNumber Field is for. So let's create an AutoNumber field and I'm going to call this "CustomerID.". Now it becomes especially important in the expert classes when we start talking about relating tables together that we have a good auto number. A good unique way of identifying each record in a table and that's what the customer id is for.

IsActive	Yes/No	On mailing list
Notes	Memo	
CustomerID	AutoNumber	

We might have 20 Johns; we could have 15 John Smith's. Phone numbers can change or be shared between customers. So the AutoNumber is really the best way of uniquely identifying each customer. It will never change and Access will automatically maintain a list for us. The first customer is 1 the second customer is 2 and so on.

AutoNumbers never get reused so we never have to worry about deleting customer 4 and then another customer 4 coming in later. People cannot edit `CustomerID`s because AutoNumbers can't be changed. So it's the perfect Field for uniquely identifying each record. In fact you don't even ever have to see AutoNumbers in your database if you don't want to. You can if you want to. You can put them on your invoices or show them in your customer Form or you can leave them completely behind the scenes and never see them.

Properly built each Table in your database should have its own AutoNumber field. The customer Table should have a `CustomerID`. The product table will have a `ProductID`. The order table should have an `OrderID`. So each Table gets its own AutoNumber Field.

Now as a matter of good design I like putting all of the ID's at the top of the Table. I just built it this way so I could show you how to move fields around. Usually when I start building a table the very first thing I do is add the ID field. But now I can show you how to move them. Take your mouse and click here on this little box to the left of where it says customer ID. Let the mouse go, that will select the entire row.

IsActive	Yes/No	On mailing list
Notes	Memo	
CustomerID	AutoNumber	

Now click again and this time drag the very top of the table, click and drag.

Notes	Memo
CustomerID	AutoNumber

You just moved a Field to the top of the Table. Again structurally Access doesn't care where in the Table the AutoNumber Field is. I personally like to have them at the top. So now that we got all the Fields in a Table let's save the Table. Let's move to the Quick Access toolbar and click the 🔲 Save button. I'm going to call mine "CustomerT" I like to end all my Tables with "T" so that it differentiated them from Queries

that I end in "Q" and of course Forms and Reports which are F and R. It's an old naming convention I've been using it many many years. Again I capitalize Customer, capitalize T, no spaces in your Table names just like your Field names for the same reasons. For consistency I like to stick with all singular Table names this way later on if I'm making a Macro or writing some VB code I don't have to go "Oh was it CustomersT or "CustomerT" I always know it's singular, again it's just a personal recommendation.

You might see some books refer to their Tables with **tbl** in front of them like "tblCustomers" that's perfectly fine too and if you're comfortable with doing that go right ahead. For me personally this is how I like to build my databases – CustomerT, ProductT, OrderT and so on.

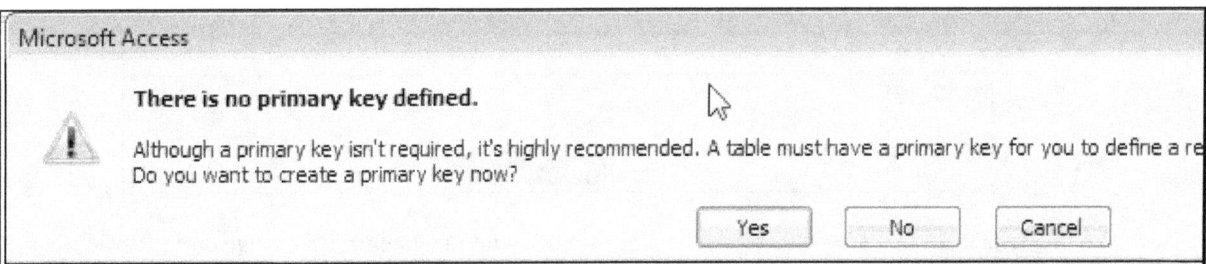

It says "There is no primary key defined although a primary key isn't required it's highly recommended." What does this primary key thing mean? Essentially a Primary Key is that one unique value that sets off each Record from every other Record. Now we've already set that up that said CustomerID but we didn't tell Access that that's a Primary Key. You can do that manually by clicking on the "Primary Key" button but I almost always forget to do it which is why I left this in the video. I want you to see that I always forget to do it. Now you know what this means. So do we want to create a Primary Key now I'll just say yes, Access sets up a Primary Key for us and you can see a little key symbol right there next to CustomerID.

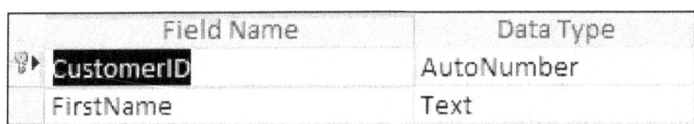

Creating a Primary Key forces that field to never have duplicate values which AutoNumbers won't anyway. Also it sets up an Index, I'll talk about that in another lesson. Now that our Tables are all set I'm going to go ahead and close it by clicking on the X and now you can see the CustomerT right here in the *Navigation Pane* all set to be opened up and have some data entered into it.

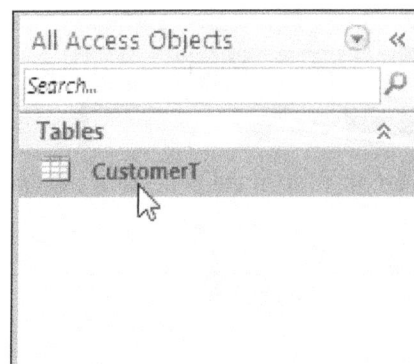

Lesson 6: Customer Table

In Lesson 6 were going to begin entering data into our Customer Table.

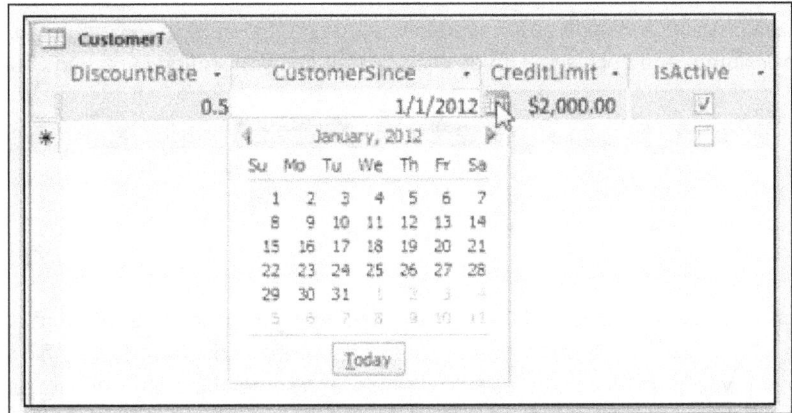

Let's go ahead now and enter in some Records into our Customer Table. Take your mouse and double-click on the `CustomerT` and that will open what we call datasheet view because it looks like the big spreadsheet zone, in `Access` they call it datasheet. Now the first Field that you will notice is the `CustomerID` and you see the word *(New)* that's our AutoNumber, as soon as they start typing in a Record into this row that *(New)* will change to the next available AutoNumber which should be 1, now press tab for the `FirstName` Field.

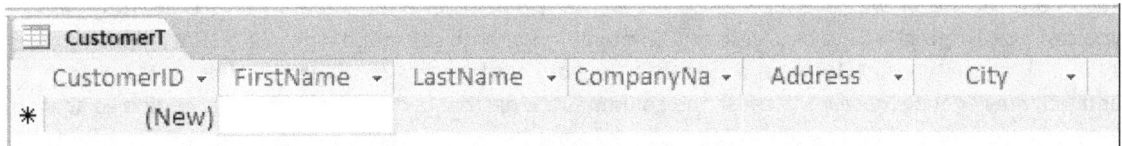

I'll type in myself, Richard, and notice as soon as I do my `CustomerID` becomes 1, I'll press tab again `LastName`, Rost, tab again, my `CompanyName` Access Learning Zone, now notice that even though the column is pretty narrow all the data will still type in there, if you want to make this wider you can just click and drag the civil boundary, click and drag to move your mouse over you get that double pointing arrow just like `Excel`, as a shortcut trick you can also double-click right here and it will resize the column exactly as wide as it needs to be to fit what data is currently in it.

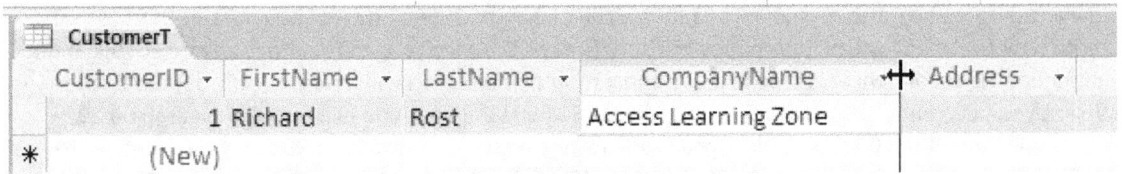

I'll press tab again put in my `Address` of the PO Box 101, tab, `City` of Amherst, `State` - New York, now I'm just going to abbriate my States with two characters, yes you can make this a drop-down box, I will teach you how to do that in a future lesson, we can pick from a list of States, that works great if you only have customers from United States and Canada but with other Countries I'll also show you a technique in our **Advanced** classes where you can pick the Country first and then only see list of States or Provinces from that Country, that's a more advanced technique we will talk about that in time, for now just type in a two digit State, tab, my `PostalCode` or `ZipCode` here in the US 14226, tab, now the `Country` Field I'm going to leave blank, if the customer is in the United States, I would say 90% of my customers are in the US and that's just fine if you leave it blank that's okay, if you want to type the Country and that's fine too I'll press tab, `Email` address I'll type in Richard.Rost@Amicron.com, notice how it comes in as a Hyperlink again I widen up, double clicking right here, if I were to click on this right now notice the little finger, that would launch my e-mail program usually Microsoft Outlook or whatever other e-mail program you happen to have installed, on my website type in www.AccessLearningZone.com and press tab again. I'll widen out that column, and once again if you click on that link you should launch in your web browser.

This brings us to the `Phone` number Field. Personally I like typing just the digits into a phone number field. Here in the US it's three for the area code, a three digit prefix and a four digit suffix, so for example 7165551212. Do not type in any parentheses () or dashes - and somewhere later on we get the formatting. I will show you how you can format that phone number to appear however you want in your Forms and Reports, for now though just type in the numbers.

This brings us to the `NumEmployees` Field. I'll type in 2 and press tab for the `DiscountRate`... I give myself a 50% discount, I'll type in 50% and press tab now notice what happens in Access just like in Excel percentages (%) are considered fractions of 1. If you type in 50% you get 0.5, 25% you get 0.25, 100% is equal to 1 so you can either type it in that way or type it in as in this case 0.5, again later on in a future class when we get to formatting numbers I'll show you how you can display that as a percentage in your Tables and moving on we have the `CustomerSince` Field. In here remember this is a Date/Time Field, you can type in either a Date or a Time or a combination of both so I could type in 11/15/11 like that and 1115 2011. I can type in 4:15 PM and I get that Time or I can type in a combination of both -11/15 5pm and tab, now I get all those #'s because the column is too narrow to display all that information so again I widen the column and there you can see all the information and Access displays Dates and Time fields again we get the formatting, I will show you how you can create a custom format to display that however you want to, for a `CustomerSince` though we don't need a Time on that so type in 3/1/90.

One one of the nice new things in Access 2010 is the added Date Picker, this little Calendar control right there, see that little box that looks like the Calendar, go ahead and click on that and you'll see a little Calendar opens up, you can scroll through the months, you can pick a day by just clicking on it, you can also jump to Today's Date and there it goes, so can use this to pick whatever Date you want.

Now a few notes on Dates, first of all in a future class I will teach you how to set a default Date so you create new records they can automatically insert Today's Date for you, a little more advanced talk about that later , the second thing is type in a day and a month and Access will automatically default to the current year, currently 2011 so if I type in 314 I get 314 2011, if you type in a two digit year in 00 29 Access will default to 2000 to 2029, if you type in a two digit year from 30 to 99 Access will default to 1930 through 1999 and so if I type in 1145 I get 1945 if I type in 1112 I get to 2012, the cutoff year is 29. Now you can change that year if you want to, it's in Windows Control Panel, it's not part of Access, it's in the regional settings portion of the control panel.

CustomerT					
NumEmployees	DiscountRate	CustomerSince	CreditLimit	IsActive	
2	0.5	3/1/1990		☐	
				☐	

Next we have the `CreditLimit`. I'll type in $2,000 notice that Access will automatically format that as a Currency for me.

`IsActive` is a checkbox you can either use your mouse and click there or if you're a keyboard person like me, I hate to stop and have to grab the mouse if I'm doing data entry, you can just use the spacebar to turn that box on and off.

Next we have the `Notes` field, you can type just about as much information you like to, "Rick is a swell guy". Now notice when I press tab I move onto the next record and Access brings me down to the next blank row while where I'm all set and ready to type in the next customer. Now a couple of quick notes before we type in anymore customers; first down here on the bottom here is the scroll bar, we can use this to scroll left and right because you can see all the data takes up more than one screenful, now the `Notes` box right here as you can see you can type a lot of information in here and you might not be able to fit it all easily on the screen so this little keyboard trick I wanna teach you it's **Shift+F2**. **Shift+F2**, that means I hold down the Shift key and press the F2 key across the top of the keyboard. When you press **Shift+F2** this Zoom window opens up, you can come in here and type as much information as you want and then when you're done hit okay and that gets saved back inside and in pretty much any field. It works extremely well for notes fields.

When we build our forms to work with this data on the screen we'll make our `Notes` field much larger so we can type more information into them without having to go in, again keep in mind when our database is built we're not going to be using the tables to enter and edit data, you never want your end users directly working with the tables and queries you want to keep them limited to just Forms and Reports so we'll make our `Notes` field big enough on our Form so we can easily edit it, right now we're the developers and we're working on building this database and personally I think it's easier to build your Forms and Reports if you already have some sample data in and that's why we're typing in some sample customer Records before we build our Forms.

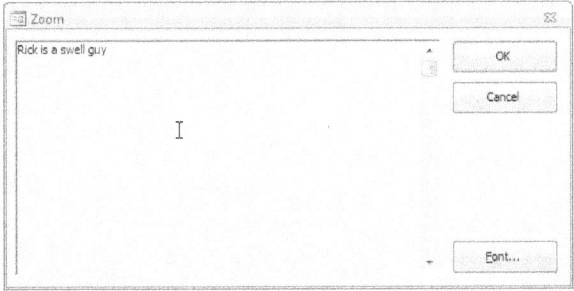

Now this click to add column over here is where you can optionally add additional Fields to your Table. I don't like using it, I like going back into Design Mode to do that, remember you can easily switch back to Table Design mode by clicking on the view button up here or drop us down and pick Design View but I'm just going to come down here and scroll back over to the left and enter in my second customer.

Lesson 7: Entering Data

In Lesson 7 we're continuing to enter data into our Customer Table.

Okay I'm ready to enter in my second Customer. I'll type in Joel Smith from XYZ Corp at 101 Main St., Buffalo, NY, 14220. I don't have his e-mail address, that's okay, I just press tab. I've always been of the mindset that it is better to have no data than they have bad data that's why I very seldom force users to have to input information. In the future class I'm going to show you how to make certain bits of information required however I almost never require users to have to type something in, you can always generate a query later that says show me all the missing data, so I can call my customers and get it, don't force your users to have to type in things like ZIP codes, what if they don't have it, they'll type in something wrong just to get the record in, same thing with website I'll tab past that, I do have his phone number 716-555-3434 tab, `NumEmployees` of say 500 tab, `DiscountRate` how about 10%, put it in as .1, that's the same as 10% tab, `CustomerSince` how about 3/1/90 tab and a `CreditLimit` of $500. `Active`? Yes. `Notes`? No notes and now I'm on to the next customer. As you can see once you've got the Table set up it's now very simple to enter in your Records.

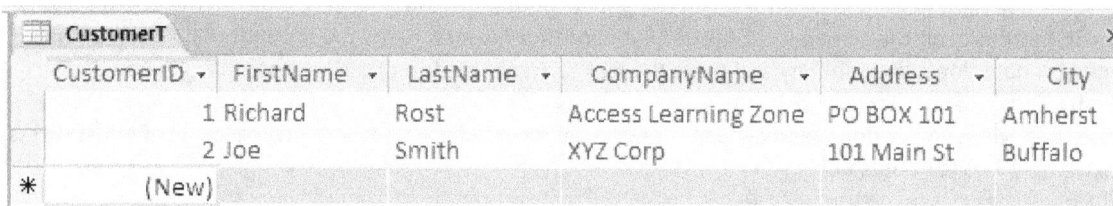

Now I'm going to type in several different customers so I've got some sample data to work with in the class. I'd like you do the same however if you don't feel like typing I'll put these sample records up on my website so you can just copy and paste them, here are my sample records if you want that in the same one that's okay just make sure you have a couple of different states or two different last names.

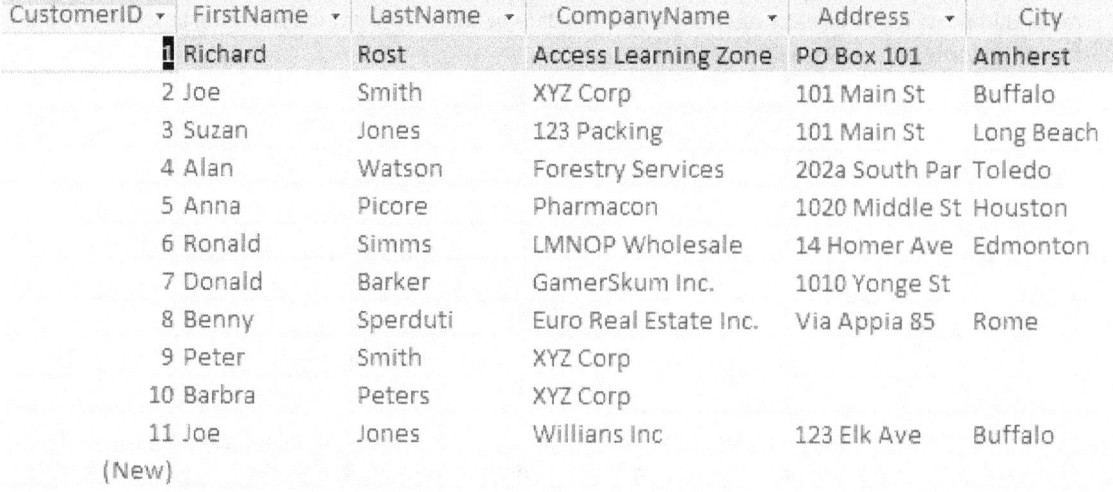

Now if you don't feel like typing and you want to use the same data I have you you can go to the special webpage and download a copy of the data, just go to 599CD.com/XACDATA1. That's a special page I just set it up, you'll find a copy of the data there, you can copy and paste right into your table.

www.599CD.com/XACDATA1

Here's the webpage, the data is right here in this little window, it's just plain text click on this button... Click to select text, that'll select it, then press **Ctrl+C** on your keyboard to Copy, that will Copy the data to your Windows clipboard, now switch back over to Access go in your Customer Table and click right here to select a new blank record. Click in the box on left hand side, see you have that arrow there that will select the entire record, you can't just be sitting like that otherwise Access will try to paste all that data into the `FirstName` field, you have to select an entire Record, right there, then hit Paste in your keyboard **Ctrl+V** as is Victor, you'll get a message that says you're about to Paste 11 Records, are you sure, go ahead and say Yes and there's the data, that's how you can Copy and Paste data between two different applications in this case your web browser and Microsoft Access.

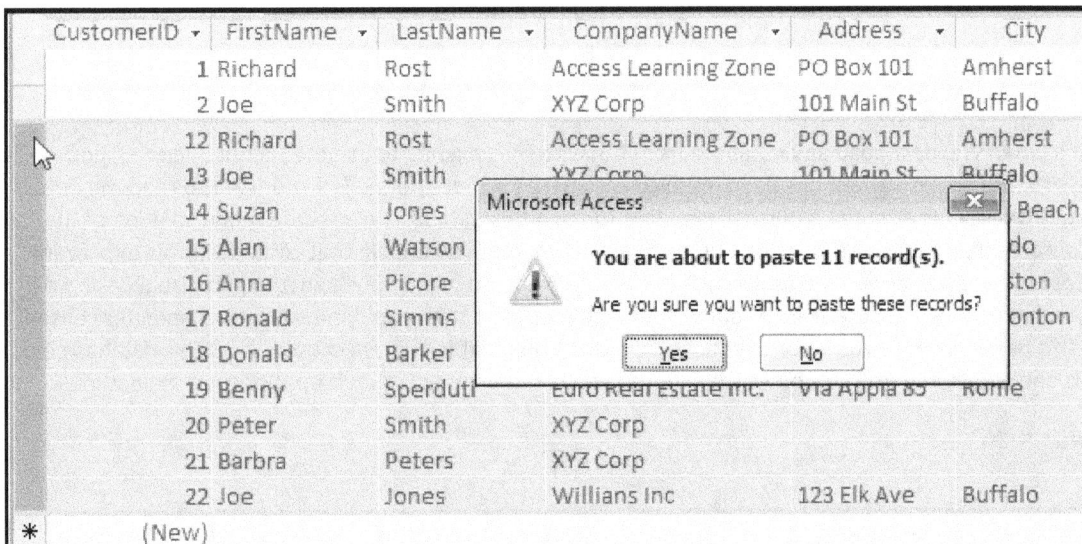

Now in this case I had already typed in these first two records so those two records are duplicated now in the database. To delete a Record just click on that same spot again, that selects an entire Record and then press Delete on your keyboard. It says "You're about to delete one record, press Yes if you're sure", press yes, now I've got two Joe Smith's, I'll just delete one of those duplicate Records, that's how you can delete a Record.

CustomerID	FirstName	LastName	CompanyName	Address	City
1	Richard	Rost	Access Learning Zone	PO Box 101	Amherst
2	Joe	Smith	XYZ Corp	101 Main St	Buffalo
12	Richard	Rost	Access Learning Zone	PO Box 101	Amherst
13	Joe	Smith	XYZ Corp	101 Main St	Buffalo
14	Suzan	Jones	123 Packing	101 Main St	Long Beach
15	Alan	Watson	Forestry Services	202a South Par	Toledo

Now don't worry if your AutoNumbers aren't the same as mine, `CustomerID`, remember we don't have to worry about the `CustomerID`, `Access` will keep track of that for us. I was playing around a little earlier copying and pasting some data, I deleted a few sample Records so as you can see here IDs 3 through 13 are now gone forever, and will never be reused but again that's okay we don't have to worry about those IDs `Access` tracks those for us. Now optionally also on the webpage I've also included a link right here to download a fresh copy of my database so if you'd rather do that instead of copying and pasting the text you can also click right here.

Step 1: Click the **button** above to select all of the sample customer records.

Step 2: Press **CONTROL-C** on your keyboard to copy those records to your clipboard

Step 3: Switch over to Access and press **CONTROL-V** to paste the records into your c table, as shown in the video.

Optionally, if you'd rather just download a copy of my **database** (ACCDB file) you ca here:

Customer Database

Now when you download any database from the web you're going to see the security warning pop-up. It says "Some active content has been disabled click here for more details". If you want to read the details you can "click here" but in a nutshell `Access` is running this database in a secure mode so none of the programming, the Visual Basic code or macros will run until you enable that content, this is to prevent people from sending you malicious code because you can do pretty much anything in Visual Basic, so if you download a database from a source you might not trust then you don't want to enable this content, in this particular case you can trust me so I'll click on the enable content button. Now this database only has one object in it, the Customer Table but as you can see when I open it up there's all my data.

Now as I mentioned in the introductory video for this course we have student forums available on the website where can post any questions you have about each lesson. If you're watching this course in our online theater you'll see the student forum for each lesson appear next to the video. Here are some of the questions that students asked about this lesson back in the `Access 2003` class:

The most popular question is "Do you have to save each record as you enter it or when you've finished entering it?", the answer is no, `Access` will automatically save each record as soon as you move off of it for example let's say I come in here and edit Anna Picore's `CompanyName` from Pharmacon to Pharacom, notice over hear in the very left-hand side this little pencil appears, that means you're in the process of editing that Record. In database terminology we call it a dirty record. Now as soon as I move off of Anna Picore's record and down to here notice the pencil goes away. Access just saved that record automatically to the table, you don't have anything more to do. When you close a table Access also saves the records.

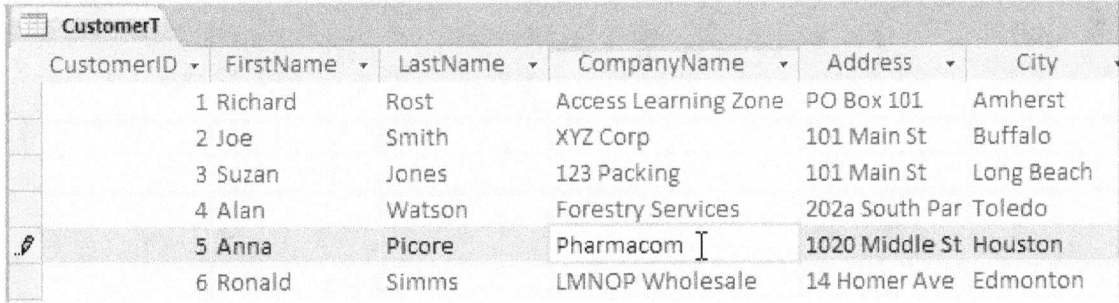

In fact the only time you actually have to save something is when you make a design change or a layout change, now a design change would be modifying one of the Fields. Changing a field name or a property type or if you make a layout change for example. If I make this column a little wider, if I go to close the table Access says do you want to save the layout of the table you can say yes and then Access will remember the width of that column, so the next time you open it will be the same width but that has nothing to do with data in the table which is saved automatically.

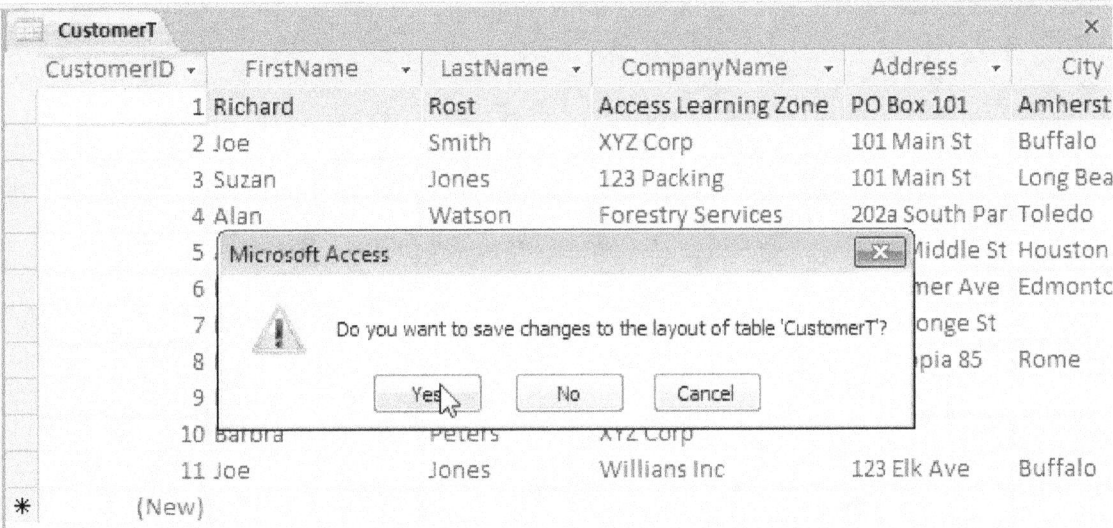

Another popular question asked is "How do you move the columns around in the table?". Well to move a column just click on the column header right here, see how I can see the down arrow, click there then let the mouse go, now click and drag, again in the same spot click and drag the left for example and now I've just moved `LastName` in front of `FirstName`, now that's another example of a layout change, it doesn't really change the structure of the table but just how the columns are displayed when you open up datasheet view, I'll move that column back to where it was by clicking and dragging it back to the right.

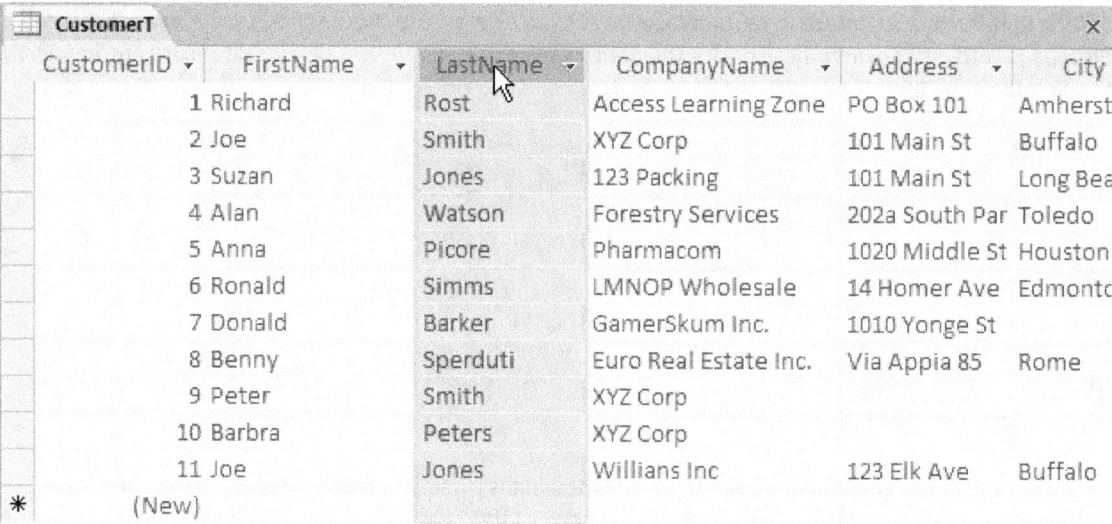

Now those are a couple examples of questions that students who have taken this course before you have asked so if you have any questions feel free to post them in the student forum window.

AccessLearningZone.com/forums

Lesson 8: Sorting & Filtering

In Lesson 8 we're going to Sort and Filter the data in our Tables.

In the last couple of classes we loaded some data into our Customer Table, right now we only have a 11 Records in our Customer Table which makes the data pretty manageable, what happens if we have 1,100 or 11,000 records in this Table then the information becomes a little more difficult to work with. Right now, for example, if I wanted to see all of the customers from New York I could just scroll over find the `State` Field and you can clearly see them here, a few more down below, if I have 11,000 customers in the Table it might not be as easy to see those customers, So what happens if the boss comes up and says all right we have 20,000 customers I want to see a list of customers only from New York Sorted by last name and I want it on my desk in 5 min, what you do?

If you're in the Table you can easily Sort or Filter your data to display just the information that you want. Sorting is pretty straightforward all you have to do is use the drop-down arrow next to the column name for example here's `LastName`, if I drop this little arrow down here you can see there is sort A-Z or Z-A. That's an Ascending or Descending Sort, so if I click sort A-Z you can see the `LastName` column is now sorted from A-Z and you can do that with any column you want, so if you want to sort by `CompanyName` just drop-down the little box, Sort A-Z and there we go that's an Alphanumeric Sort.

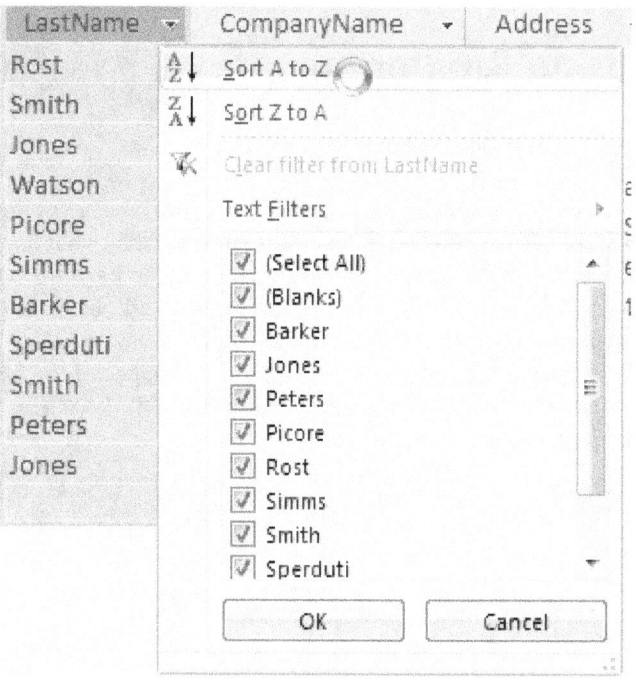

If you sort a column like State here and that has missing values, also called null values, drop that down and sort A-Z, you can see that the empty or null value show up at the top of the list:

If you sort a numeric field like NumEmployees you see it says Sort Smallest to Largest or Largest to Smallest:

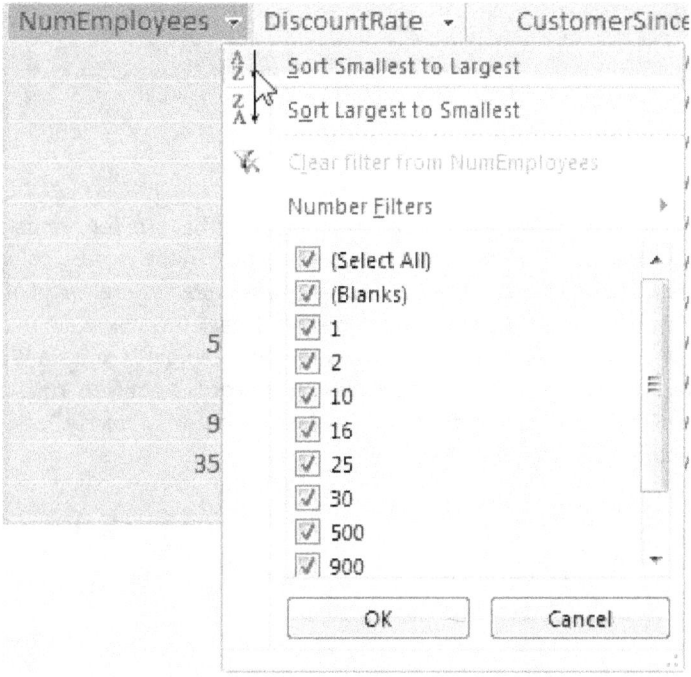

A Date/Time field by `CustomerSince` you can Sort Oldest to Newest or Newest to Oldest:

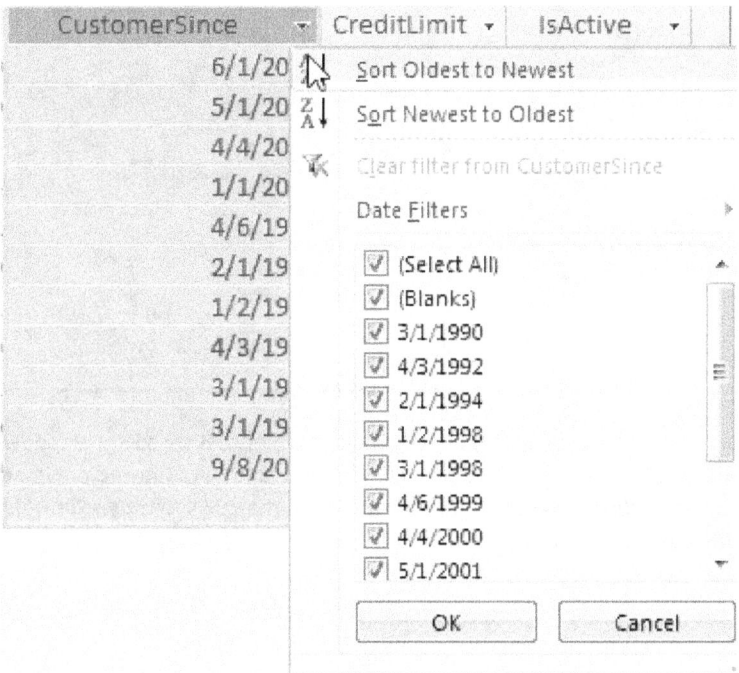

Now there are some advanced techniques with Table Sorting, we will talk about those in future classes, you can do things like setting up multicolumn Sorts, but for now on the *Home* tab come up here and click on Remove Sort in the Sort and Filter group that will clear whatever sorts you have on there.

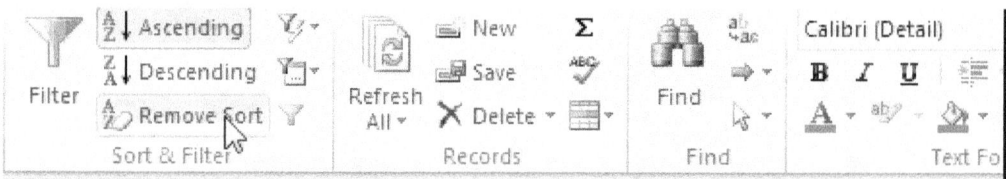

You can also Filter your data to show just a subset of the Records that are, for example, the boss only wants to see Companies that are from New York. So come up here in the `State` column drop the box down and you'll see down here a bunch of filters. There are checkboxes here for all of the different items that are in that list, right now all of the items are selected. If I check this box again that says (Select All) it turns them all off. Now you can pick individual items to see, for example, if you want to see just the blank Records or just the Records from New York or perhaps even Records from New York and Ohio, but the boss only wants to see Records from New York so I'll make sure just that box is checked on then I'll hit OK and now you can see our results are filtered:

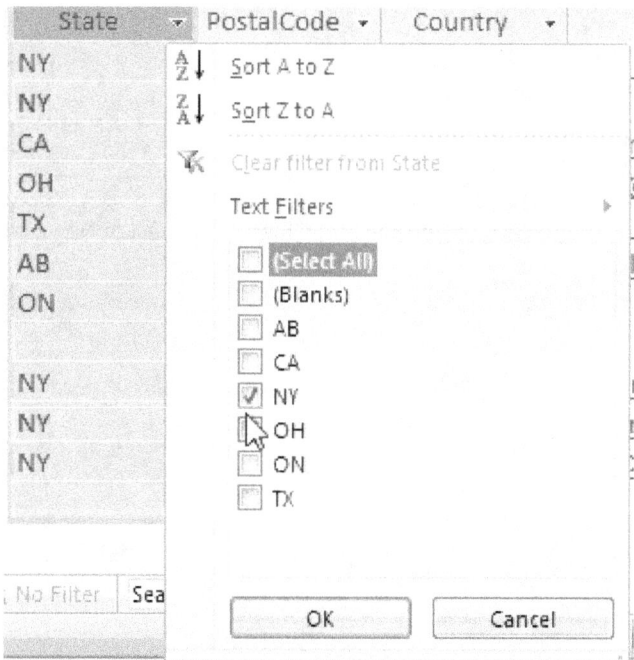

You can tell when a filter is on a couple of different ways, right here it says Filtered, down here in the *Status Bar* it says Filtered, this little symbol appears right here that says filtered or `State` equals New York, even up here on the *Ribbon* that little guy is highlighted that says Remove Filter, just click on that to remove the Filter, just like this one or most sort.

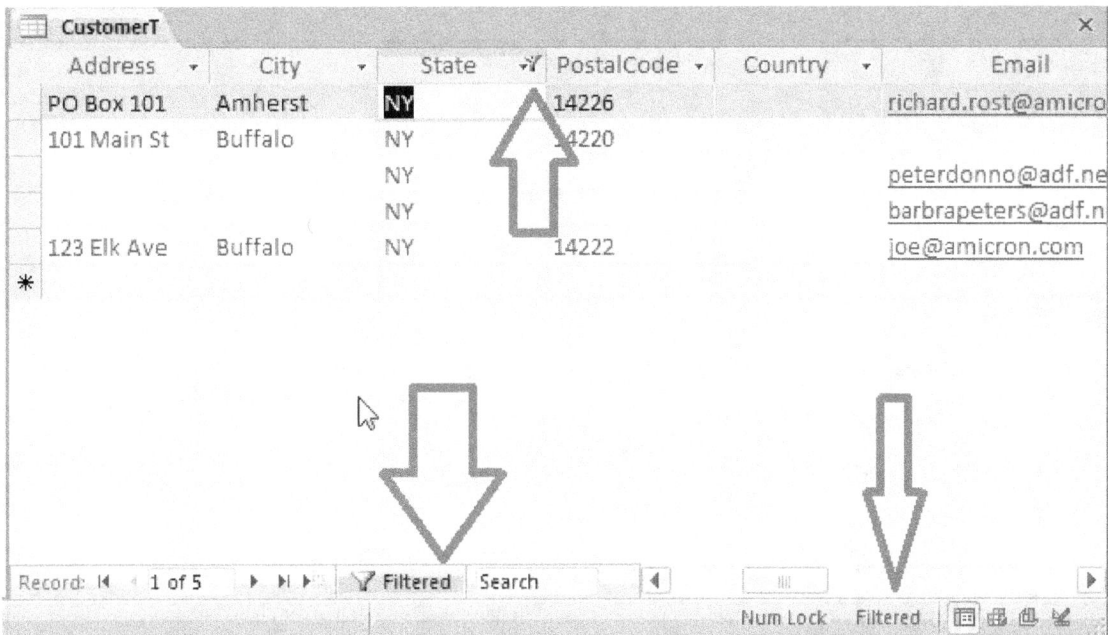

Additionally if you look down here these are what are called *Navigation Buttons*, we will talk more about these when we get to Forms. You can see it says 1 of 5 now instead of 1 of 11. That's how we can tell we are dealing with a filtered set of Records. Now yes you can apply multiple Filters, you could Filter by `State` and then `ZIPCode` inside of that `State`, you can apply a Filter and then a Sort, for example right now we have just our customers from New York so now I can come over here and then Sort by `LastName`. Now I have the results the boss wanted, all the Customers from New York sorted by `LastName` so I could print this out.

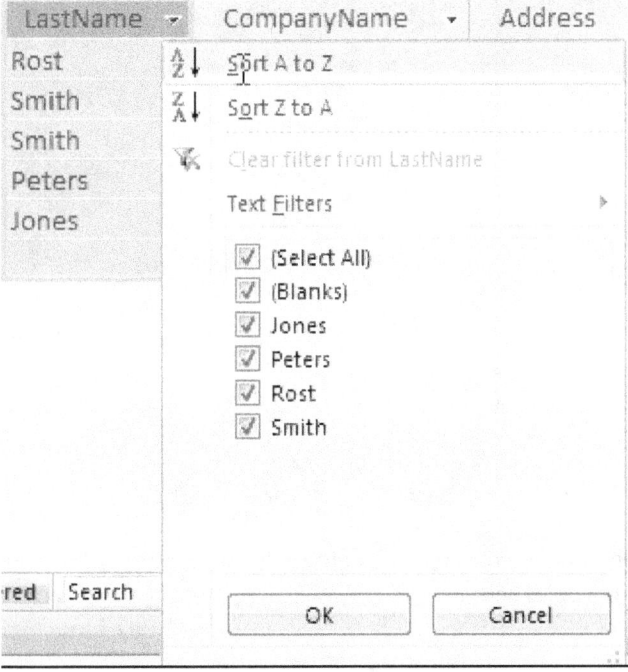

Click on File

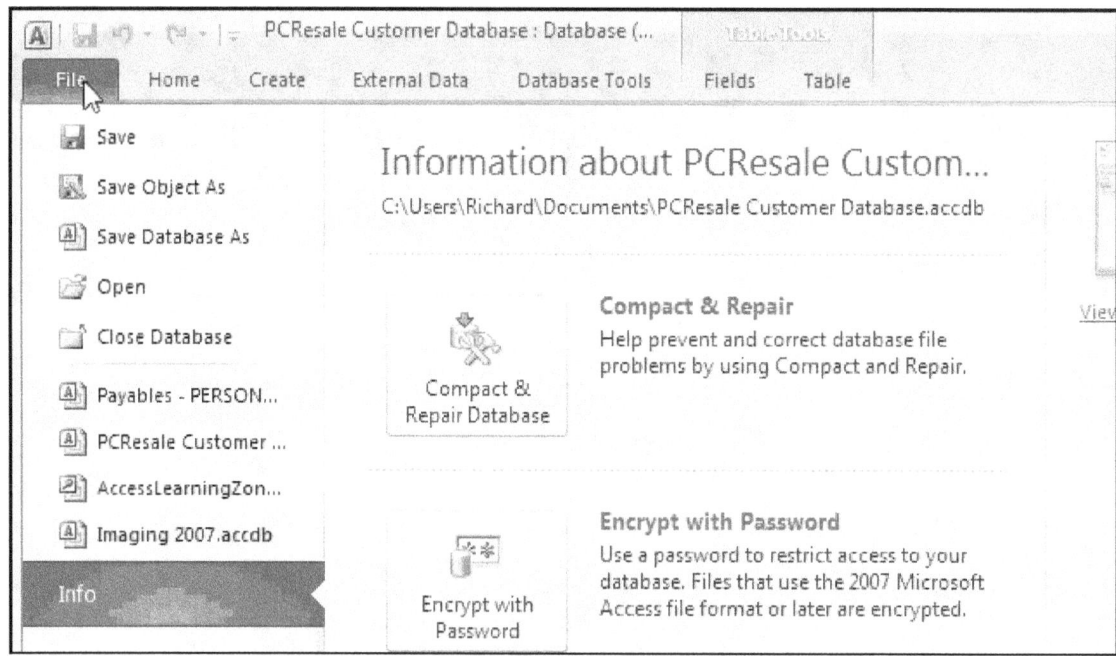

To print out a Table and while come down to the bottom, Pick Print

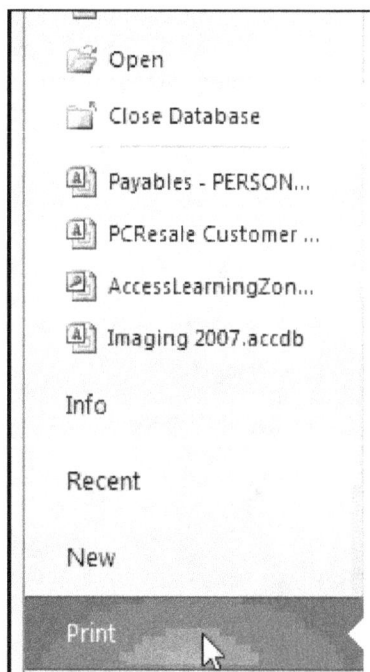

and then select either Quick Print which sends it right to the printer or the Print option which lets you pick the printer, the number of copies and so on.

Print

Quick Print
Send the object directly to the default printer without making changes.

Print
Select a printer, number of copies, and other printing options before printing.

Print Preview
Preview and make changes to pages before printing.

Now Sorting and Filtering are okay for you as the Developer, remember we never want other people to use our Tables directly, there's just too much room for too many problems to creep into your database. You don't want end-users playing with your Tables, this is fine if you just want to get in here maybe take a look at some Records, see some things a different way, Sort some stuff, that's fine for you but not your end users. Also you can't rely on Access to save your Sorts and Filters in the Table, so if you have multiple sets of data that you have to be able to generate these Reports on a regular basis you don't want to constantly keep coming back to the Table to reapply Filters and Sorts, Let's say today you need a list of Customers from New York sorted by `LastName`, tomorrow you might need a list of customers from Pennsylvania with $5000 or greater `CreditLimits`, the next day a list of customers from California who've been with you for at least a year. You want to be able to generate all these different kinds of lists of customers without having to come back into the Table to make changes, that's what Queries are good for. You can set up a Query once, customers from New York sorted by `LastName` save that as a Query then in the future if you want to run that again you just open up the Query and the work is already done.

So in the next lesson we will learn how to set up a Query to do exactly what we just did with the Table, however the Query can be saved for future use.

Lesson 9: Queries

In Lesson 9 were going to learn how to build Queries, apply a Multi-Field Sort to the Query and a Criteria Filter.

In this lesson we have the same mission that we had in the last lesson, the boss wants a list of customers from New York State sorted by my `LastName`, more importantly I want to create a Query to do this so I can pull it up at a moments notice anytime in the future.

To create a Query click on the *Create* tab and over here under the Queries section you'll see a Query Wizard and then Query Design. Now the Query Wizard is okay for making some of the more advanced Queries but we're only going to make a very simple Query right now and I want teach you how to do this from scratch, so come over here and click Query Design.

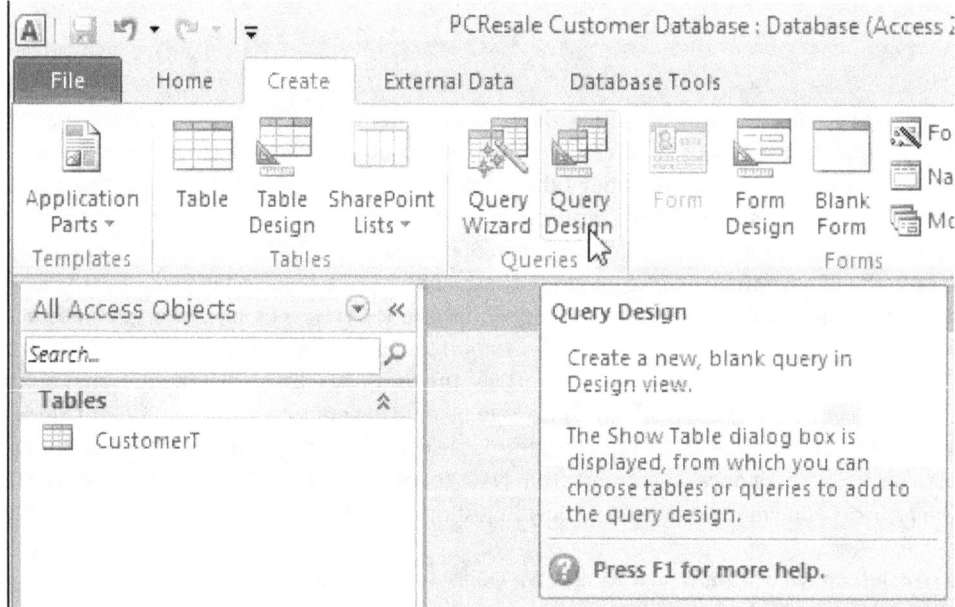

The first thing that you'll see is a blank Query in the background, right now it says *Query1* and you'll see the Show Table window, now a Query can get data from one or more Tables or one or more other Queries or you can see a list of both of them. Now we only have one Table in our database right now so that's the only thing we can pull data from but later on when we have multiple Tables and different Queries we can actually build Queries off of all of those things, for now to keep it simple lets just click on `CustomerT`, click on the Add button and you'll notice the `CustomerT` goes into the Query back here. Now if I had additional Tables or Queries that I wanted to add I could do that now but I don't, just the one Table is fine, click on close and now you're in the Query.

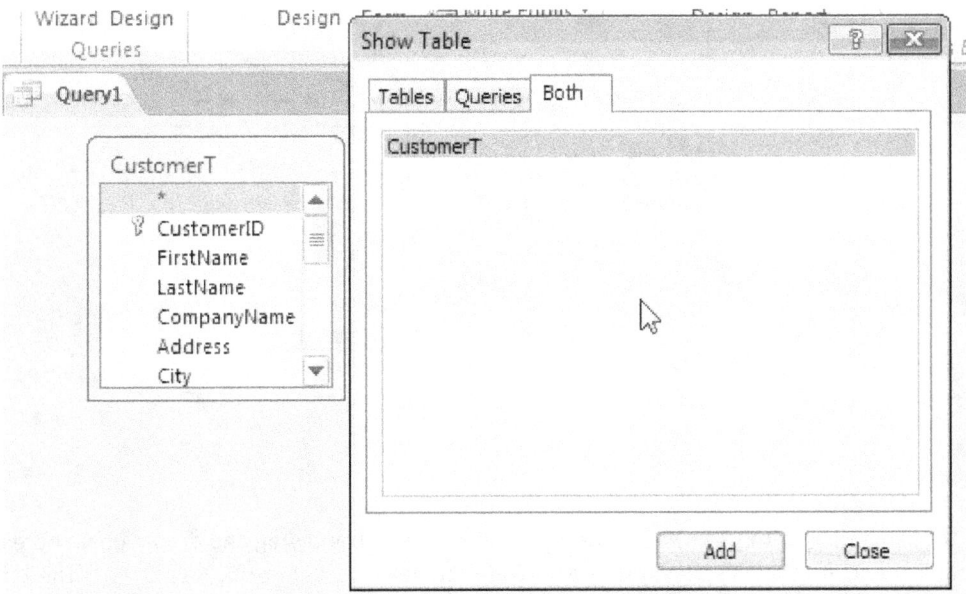

Down below under here you'll see different columns on the left-hand side it says Field; Table; Sort; Show; Criteria and Or; Now I will tell you this is one of the stranger things you'll see in Access. This is one of the weirdest screens to understand but once you get the hang of it it's really quite simple. Basically it works like this, up here is the Table that we're getting the data from, down here are the Fields or columns for the Query, so essentially we take the information we want to see from the Table and bring it down below.

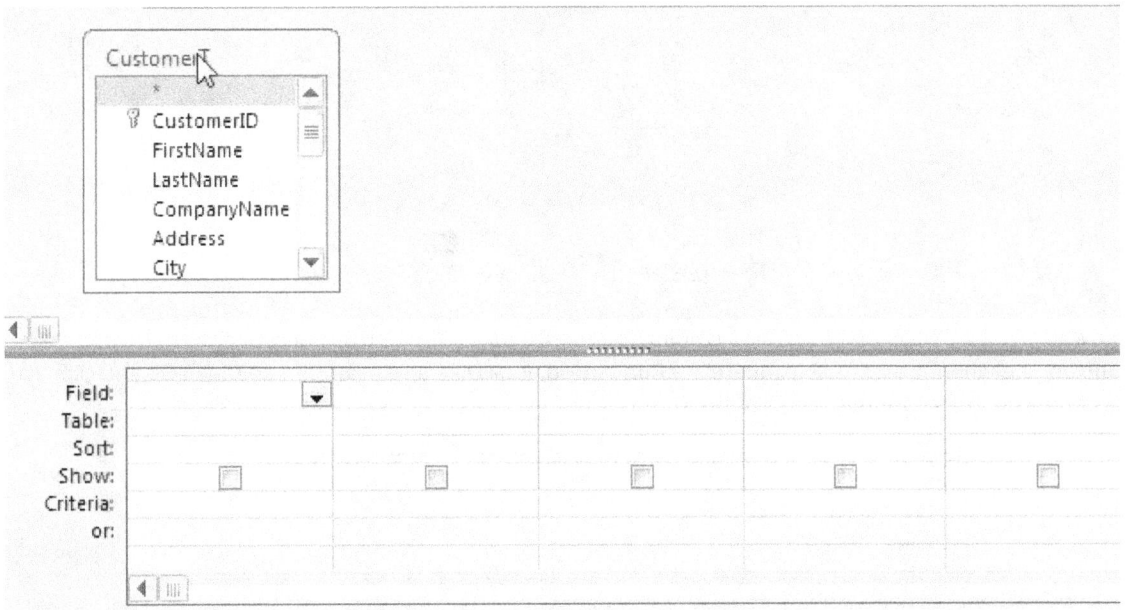

So let's say I want to see `FirstName` and `LastName` in my query, click and drag `FirstName` and drop it right down here in the first column:

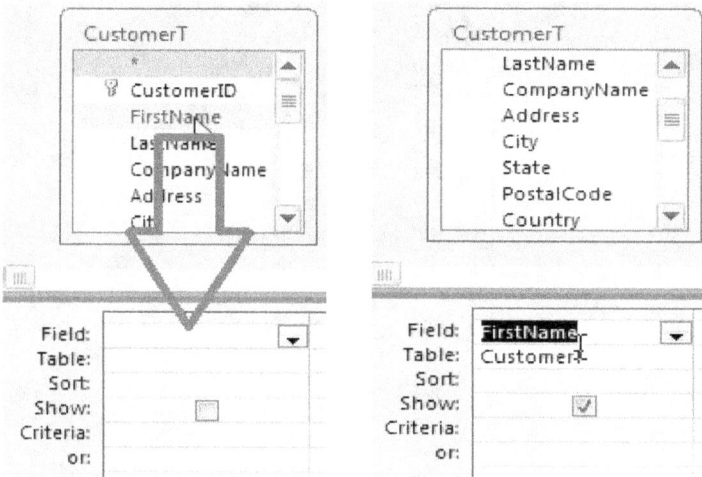

Now do the same thing with `LastName`, there's `LastName` click and drag and drop it down here into the second column, it's that easy, you can see here are the fields `FirstName`, `LastName`, the Table they are from shows up, down below here we only have one Table right now, if you had multiple Tables you might see different Table names down here and that's how you put fields in your Query, it's very simple.

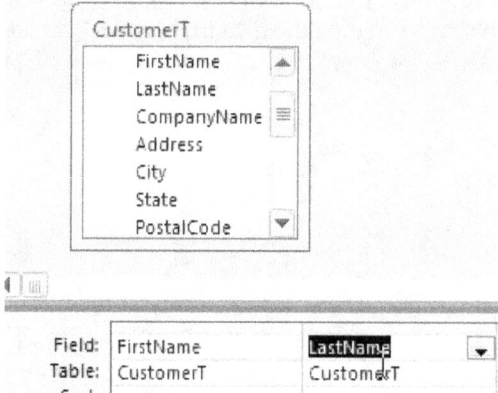

Now to see the results that the Query is going to produce take your mouse and click right here on the Run button, see where it says Results, there is a Run button, looks like an exclamtion point (!). Go and click on that now and there are the results of the Query.

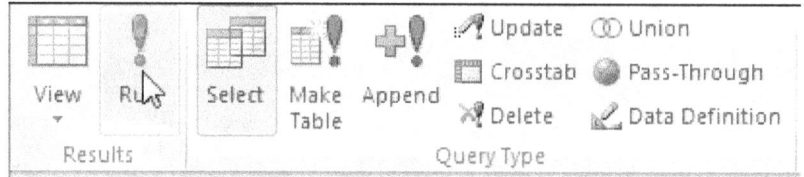

Now all I asked for at this point was to show me a list of all the Customer's `FirstName` and `LastName`. That it's not sorted yet there's no filter, I just told the Query show me all the Customers, show me `FirstName` and `LastName`, `Access` gave us exactly what we asked for:

Let's say in addition to `FirstName` and `LastName` I also want to see the `Phone` number. Perhaps the reason the boss wants this list it to have someone call all these customers, so lets add `Phone` number to this Query. First we need to go back into Design View, remember when we were working on our Table we had Datasheet View and Design View, same thing over here there's our button to go back into Design View, you drop this down, you see the Datasheet View, a couple of other views are in here don't worry about those for now and there is Design View, click on Design View and it puts you back into the Query.

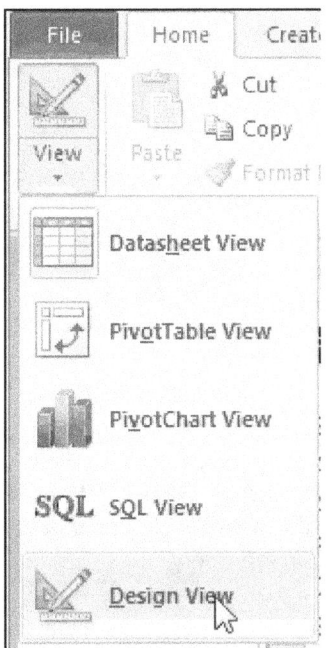

So to add another Field, just find it up here in the Table where his `Phone` number, there it is right there, now here's a trick you can click and drag it like I showed you earlier or just double-click on it, watch this, click click and there it goes, it drops right down there into the next column:

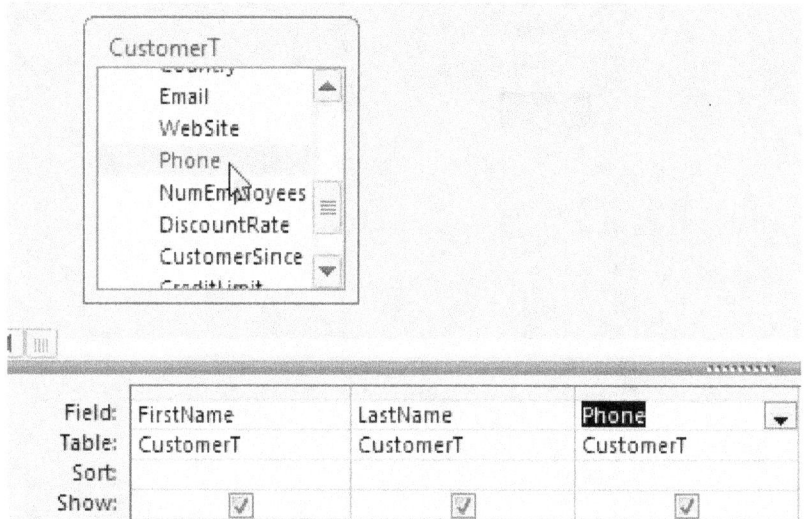

Now go ahead and run your Query again and you'll see `FirstName`, `LastName` and now `Phone` number.

FirstName	LastName	Phone
Richard	Rost	7165551212
Joe	Smith	7165553434
Suzan	Jones	5624365146
Alan	Watson	4193895477
Anna	Picore	7132364479
Ronald	Simms	7807465468
Donald	Barker	4164415555
Benny	Sperduti	7167267262
Peter	Smith	5645597777
Barbra	Peters	8292827288

The Query will display just the information that you want to see.

Now how do we Sort this information, well we could use the same Sort and Filter buttons right here in the Datasheet View but those don't necessarily get saved with the Query. Here's what I want you to do, go back into Design Mode and right down under here under the Field name you'll see there's a Sort row, this is where we specify the Sort for the Query, so for example let's say I want to Sort by `FirstName`, click inside this box, here you see by a drop-down arrow, click on that, there is Ascending; Descending and (Not Sorted); Let's pick Ascending and now run the Query (!).

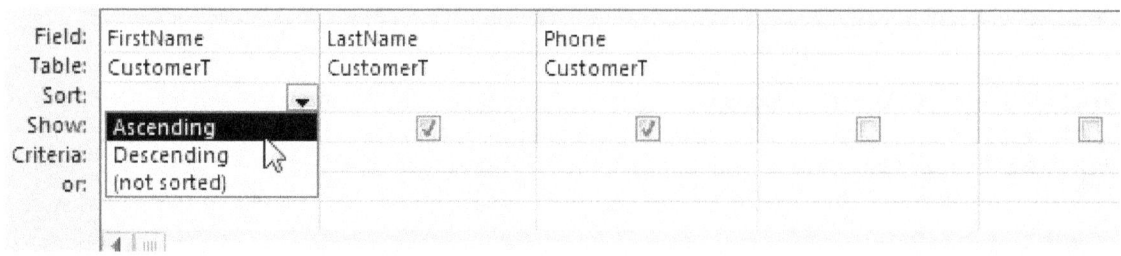

Notice the results are sorted by FirstName.

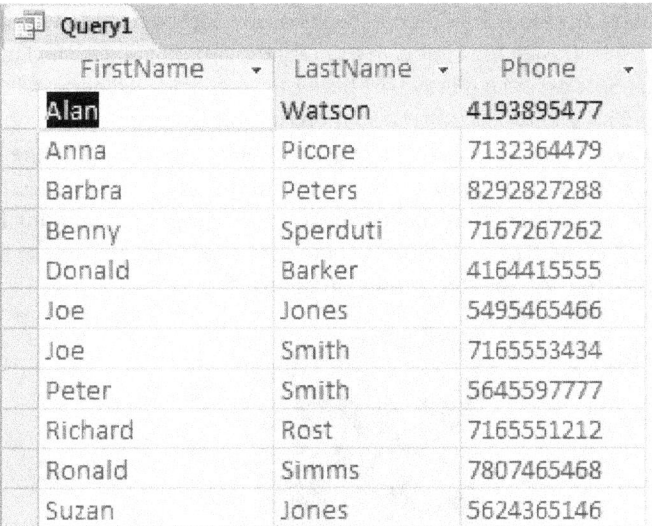

Alright back to Design View, if you want to Sort by LastName first turn this Sort off, say (Not Sorted) and then Sort only by LastName and now run the Query (!).

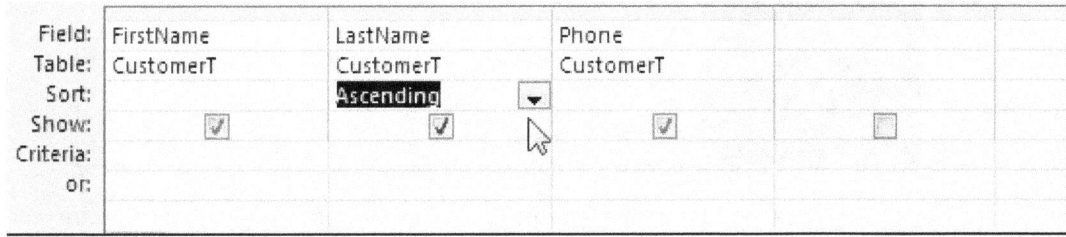

Now its sorted just by LastName:

Now what I'd like to happen is to have the records Sorted by `LastName` and then `FirstName`, so if their last names are the same the Records would then be in Sort order based on their first name which in this particular case for the Jones' that did work, Joe came on top of Susan however the Smiths' are backwards Peter should be after Joe, but I didn't specify as my Sort so how do we Sort by more than one column, well come back into Design View, now in a Query the order in which the Fields appear from left to right determines their Sort order so if I say Sort both of these Fields Ascending `FirstName` will get sorted first and then `LastName` will get sorted so then run this Query now you can see it sorted by `FirstName` and then by `LastName` but that's not what I want, come back to the Design View, in order to get `LastName` to sort first I have to move `LastName` to the left in Design Mode, so come down here, move right over this gray bar, on top of the column you'll see a downward pointing black arrow, click right there and let the mouse go now click on the exact same spot and drag your mouse to the left and that will move the column, just like moving columns around in tables.

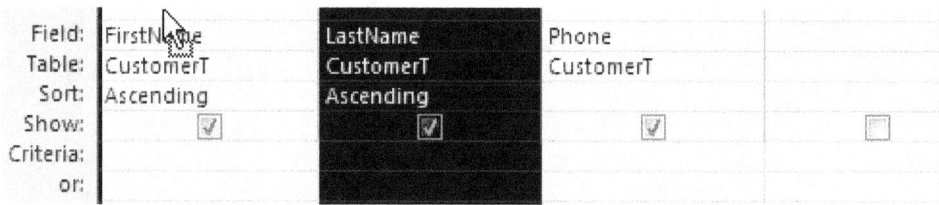

Now `LastName` will be sorted before `FirstName` is sorted:

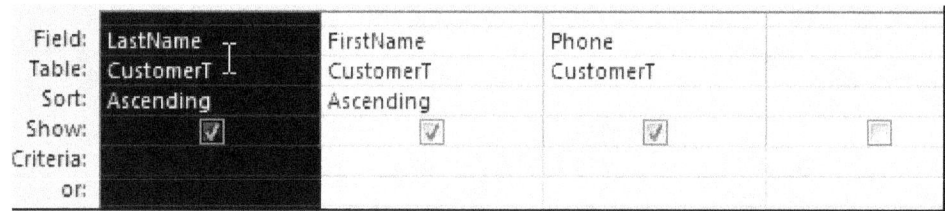

So if I run the Query now that's the Sort that I'm looking for, Sorted by `LastName` and then where two last names are the same it's sorted by `FirstName`, so that's how you do a Multi-Column Sort.

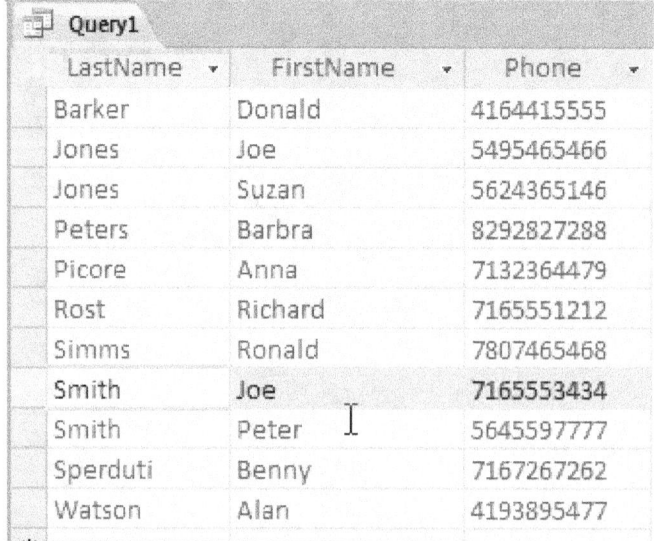

Okay back to Design View, now let's save our Query. This is the major benefit of using Queries as we can save this and not have to do any of this work again in the future to get the same list of customers, so I'll come up top and click on the  Save button on the Quick Access toolbar or you can see there by the control tip text that says **Ctrl+S**, **Ctrl+S**, a keyboard shortcut that you can press that will also save the Query.

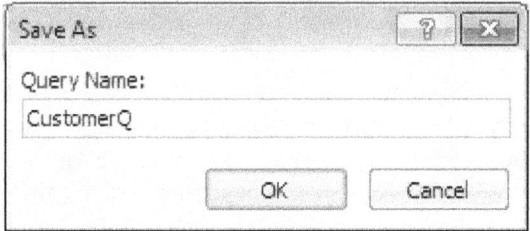

The SaveAs dialog box appears, I'm going to say this as my `CustomerQ`, no space in there, `CustomerQ`, Q stands for Query and click OK:

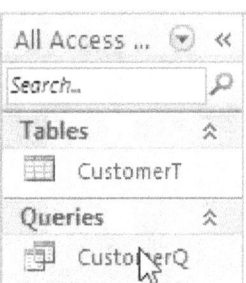

Notice the `CustomerQ` appears over here in the *Navigation Pane* and we now have a new section called Queries. `CustomerQ` appears here on the tab as well. Now if I close the Query all I have to do in the future to run it to get the same set of Customers is just double click on my `CustomerQ` and there it is.

Now we're not finished with our Customer Query just yet because the boss said I only want to see Customers from New York, we have to somehow filter this list based on the `State` so go back to Design View. How do we filter based on the `State`? Well first we have to get the `State` Field into our Query, that's easy to do, we already know how to do that, scroll down the Field list, right here and find the `State` field, then I'll double click on it, now I've added the `State` field to the Query:

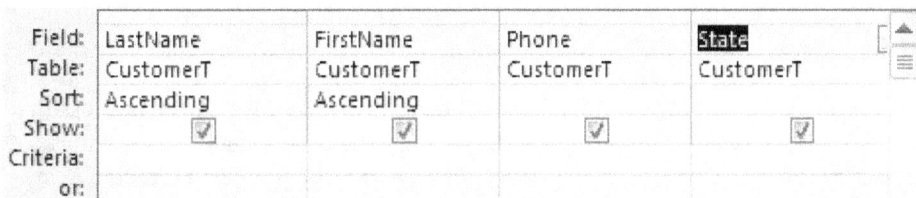

If I run the Query right now you'll see there are all the `States`.
Now I haven't filtered it yet, again we could cheat and come up here and apply a filter right here but these don't reliably get saved in the Query.

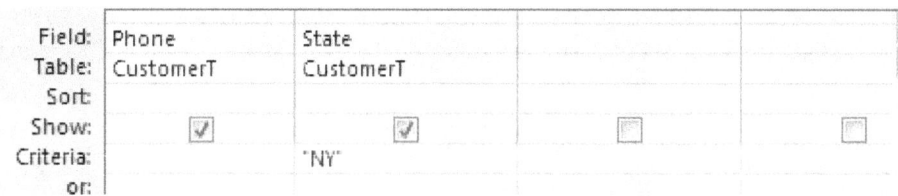

So go back into Design Mode and down here you'll see a row that says Criteria. The Criteria row is essentially a Filter for the Query so I'm going to come down here under `State` in the Criteria row and I'm going to type in an "NY" for New York, then press tab, that moves me over to the right and look what happens New York has quotes around it. Now that's fine, basically saying that New York is a text value as opposed to a Number value or a Date value, that's what I want, we will talk more about what those quotes mean exactly in future lessons.

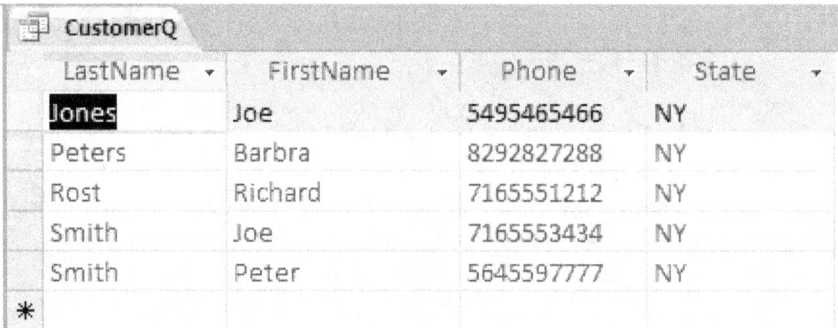

But now I've set up a Criteria that the `State` has to be equal to "NY". Now go-ahead run the query again and there you can see just the Customers from New York are displayed:

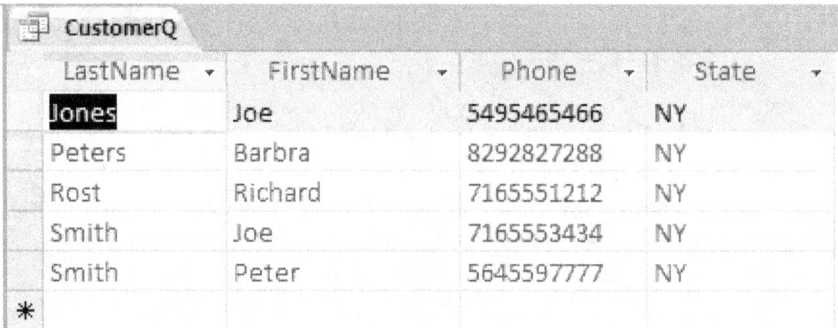

Now I want to save this Query but don't just click on the floppy disk 💾 Save button because that's the save command, it will save this Customer Queuy over the old Customer Queue, let's use the 📄 SaveAs command so we can change the name of the Query. This is a trick that I show my student in my Microsoft Word class, if you're working on a document, say a letter and you're writing a letter to Joe Smith and you want to send the same letter to Sue Jones you open it up make a few changes go File | 📄 SaveAs and change the filename, the same thing works in here for database objects and of instead of clicking on the

Save button we're going to go to File and then "Save Object As", alright save 'CustomerQ' to:, the default is "Copy of CustomerQ" I'm gonna change this to "CustomersFromNYQ" just like that.

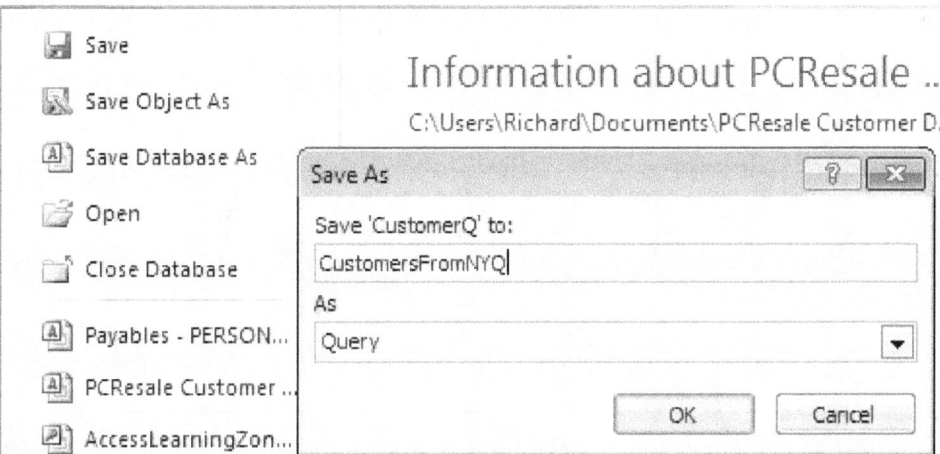

And then I'll hit OK, the object is saved, now click on the File tab again to close that down and here you can see open this up a little bit, here you can see both of our Queries: `CustomersFromNY` and our old `CustomerQ`.

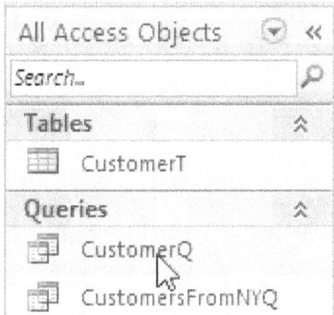

You can open up the other one by double-clicking on it, notice here I now have two tabs, they're both open at the same time, there's `CustomersFromNY` and just the `CustomersQ`, I'll close that one and close this one, and then see now how I can open up both of these at any time in the future without having to do any more work. The Sort and Filter or should I say the Criteria is saved in the Query.

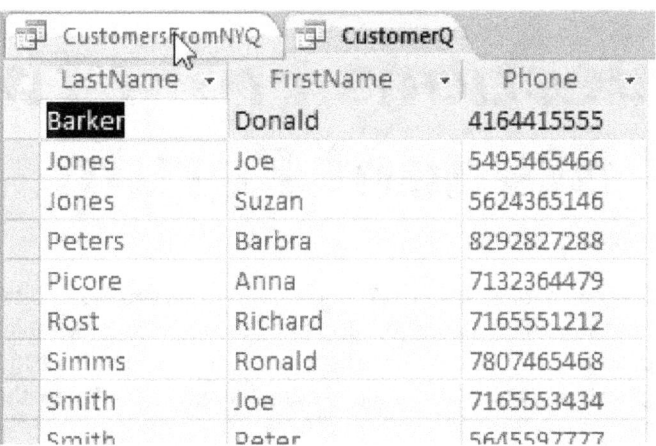

Now if you want to make a change to this Query, let's say you want to save this as "`CustomersFromPA`" all you have to do is go into Design View and find your Criteria, which is right over here, double-click, I'll change that to "PA" (Pennsylvania), I'll go to File |  Save Object As, change this to `CustomersFromPAQ`, hit OK,

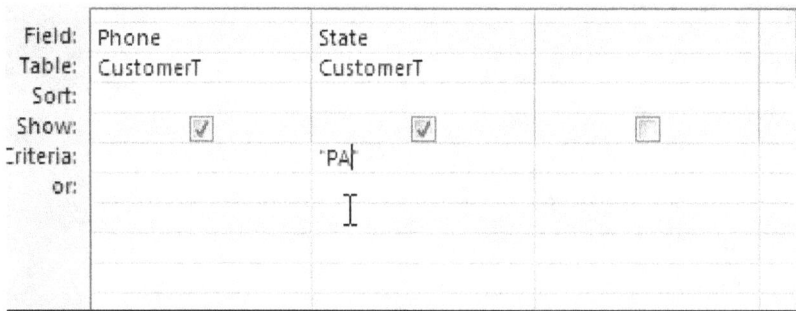

Close the File tab and now you can see I multiple Queries over here:

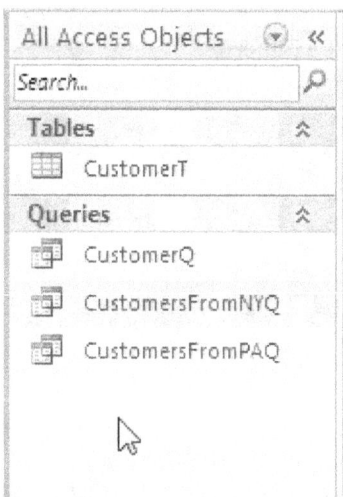

Now it's time for some questions from the Student Forum, these are questions that previous students have had about the material on this lesson.

Questions From The Student Forum

The first question is "Can I edit data in the query?" The answer is yes you most certainly can. Remember Queries themselves do not store data they're just displaying the data from the table in a different way so even though you're only seeing `LastName`, `FirstName`, `Phone` number here you can come in here and change these things so be very careful, don't make any changes in the Query that you wouldn't make in the Table.

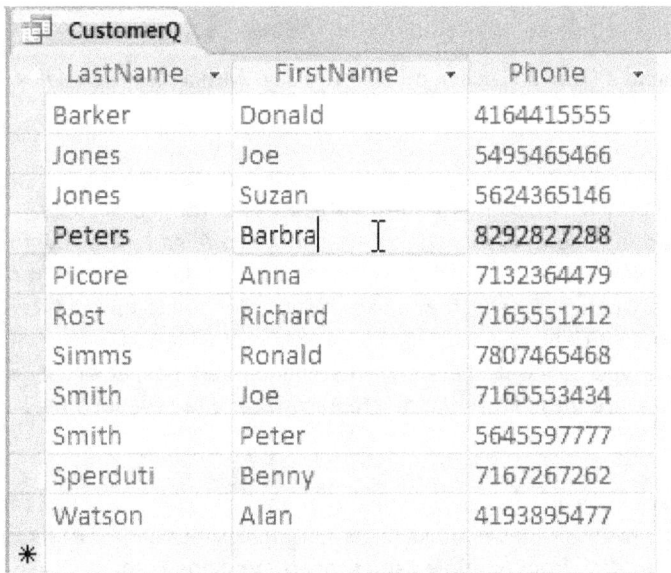
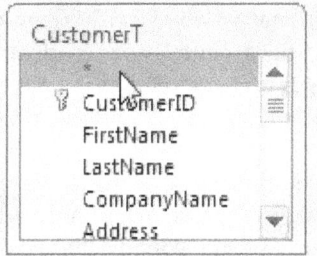

The next question "If I wanted to make a Report for each State would I have to make 50 separate Queries?"

The answer of course is no, I'm just showing you the very basics of Query design right now, later on I'm going to teach you how to create something called a Parameter Query where you can set up a Query that the user types in the `State` that he wants to see when he runs the Query. So we'll open the Query up, it'll say enter the `State`, type in "NY" and there's the Records from New York, close it down. Again and type in "CA" and you'll see California, that's called a Parameter Query and we will cover that in a future lesson.

Finally another popular question "what is this "*" on top of the list of customer fields?"

The "*" is something you can add to the Query if you want to see all of the Fields displayed every time the Query runs, this way you can bring in the Fields that you want to Sort or put criteria's on and then add the "*" in to see all the rest of them and again we will talk about this in more detail in a future lesson.

So now we know how to build Tables and simple Queries in the next lesson will start working on Forms.

Lesson 10: Forms

In Lesson 10 we're going to learn how to build a Form so we can present our user with a nice friendly interface for editing records.

So far today we've seen how to build a Table and how to design a couple of different Queries. Now Tables and Queries are functional and they're necessary for most databases but they're not very user-friendly to work with especially if you don't know Access so in this lesson we're going to see how to set up a couple of different types of Forms. Now Forms are used to work with data on the screen. Forms look a lot better than working with Tables & Queries directly, that makes it easier for you to find information which of course makes you more efficient with your database. Forms provide you with additional control and security for your data, you can control exactly where people can look, at which Fields they can see, which ones they can add, are they allowed to delete Records or add new Records, all these things can be controlled using Forms.

If you currently have paper Forms or perhaps even an Excel spreadsheet that you're working with you can design a Form to mimic those existing paper forms or Excel spreadsheets, this makes it easier for users to transition into your database. You can display data from multiple Tables together on one Form, for example you can show the contact history for each customer on the Customer Form. We can show a summary of the recent orders. We're not going learn how to do that today but just keep in mind we can do it and will cover that when we get to our **Expert** classes and start talking about Relational Tables. Forms can display summary information, if you have a Form that shows a list of orders you can put totals in the footer of the Form so at the bottom of the column you can see the total for all the orders.

In today's class I'm going to show you how to set up a couple of different simple Forms using some of the automatic form techniques. We'll show you how to make some basic modifications to those Forms as well. In the next level we'll spend a lot more time designing custom Forms from scratch, keep in mind that building Forms is really more of an art than a science, you can easily spend many many hours making your Forms look good, I know that I have in the past. Changing round the controls, where they go, changing the colors, it just takes practice; This is something that the more you do it the better you become.

So here is how you create a simple Form. First click on the Table or Query that you wish to base your Form on. Generally you're going to base your forms directly from your Tables however if you wish to show a custom set of Records you can build a Form directly from a Query, we'll show you how to do that in a custom lesson.

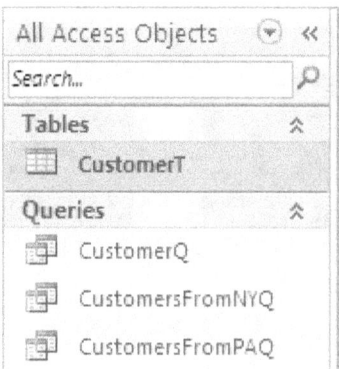

For now we're gonna click on Customer Table, click on Create and then over here you'll see the Forms group. There are several different ways to build a Form in Access, the simplest is just to click on the Form and Access will go ahead and build a Form for you, it won't give you any options, it will just say here you go there's your Form. I'll show you how that works in just a minute.

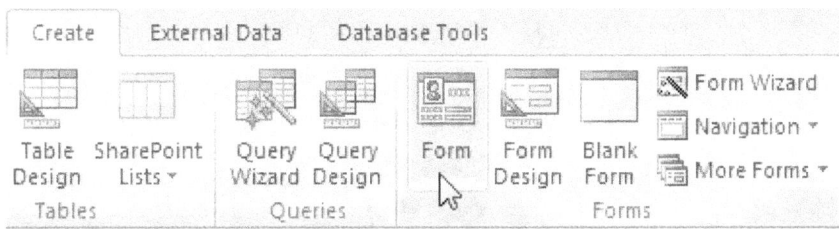

Next we have Form Design, which is you building the Form from scratch. Now Form Design is actually my preferred method for building Forms, however it's a little more advanced and we're going to cover that in the next class. Form Design lets you really get in there and make changes to every aspect of the Form but you have to know how to build them from the ground up so again we'll cover that in the next class.

Blank Form will build the Form for you and then lets you add the controls where you want them, again we will see this in the future lesson in.

The Form Wizard will help you to build a Form by asking you some simple questions; you can then customize the Form once it's been built. I personally don't like the Form Wizard and will cover this in a future lesson.

Navigation allows you to set up a simple menu interface with buttons, where you can click on them to go between the different parts of your database.

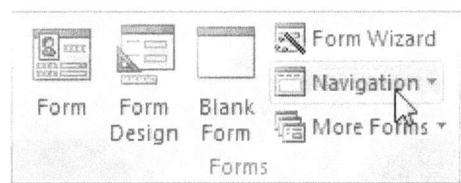

And then under More Forms there are some different optional types of Forms. We will see a couple of these today like Multiple Items, Datasheet and Split Form, we will talk about the others in future classes.

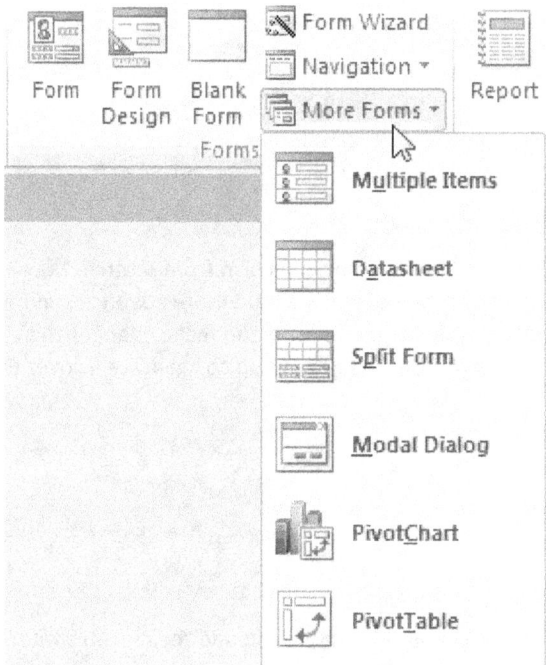

So as you can see there are a lot of different options available for Forms but for now let's just click on the simple Form here. When you click on it a second goes by and then Access throws together the Form for you. On the Form you'll see a header across the top, here that says CustomerT, then you'll see each one of the Fields from your Table down below, here is `FirstName` and `LastName` and so on, this is called a Single Form because each screenful shows one Record, a single Record at a time, you can see each field consists of a Label and a Textbox. The Label is right here on the left, it indicates which Field this is. On the right side you'll see the Textbox, this is where the actual data goes.

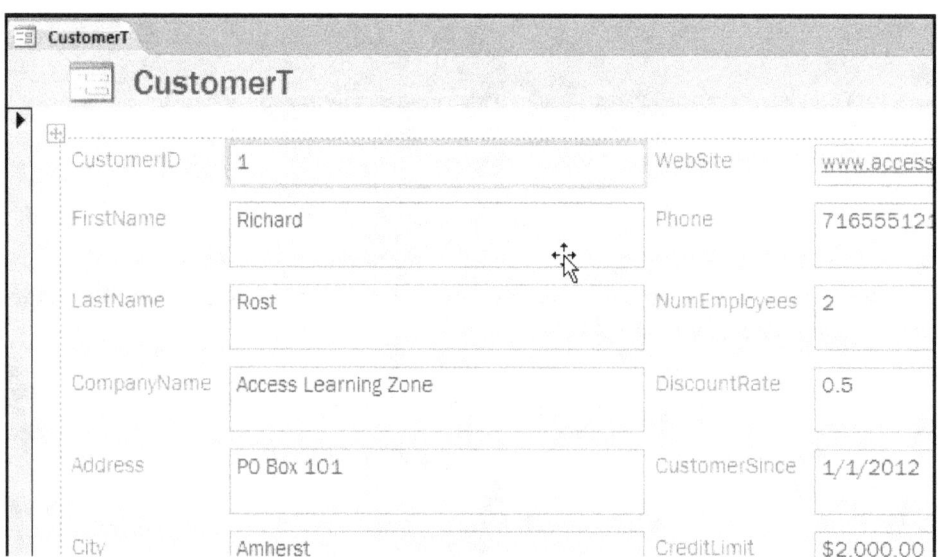

Now when Access first builds the Form for you it puts you inside of Layout Mode, what that means is you can come in here and change the layout of the Form to look like whatever you want, you'll see up top here it says *Form Layout Tools*, we can change the design, the arrangement and the format of the Form.

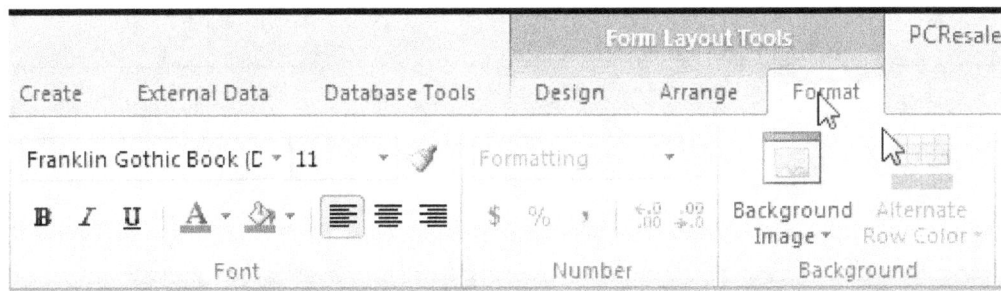

If you click on the *Design* tab, way over here in the left you'll see views, just like we had with Tables and Queries, if you drop this down you'll see there is Form View, Layout View and Design View, right now we're in Layout View. You can see that Layout View has a little orange border around it, this means we can edit the layout of the Form. Once we're happy with the layout we can switch to Form View and that's where we can actually edit our data, that is what your end-users will be working with all the time, Form View, you don't want to let them mess with your layout or your design. Now Design View we will talk about in next class. Design View lets you get in there and make changes to the properties of the objects, move things around a little bit more and basically make more changes than you can with just editing the layout, we will talk about that, again, in the next class.

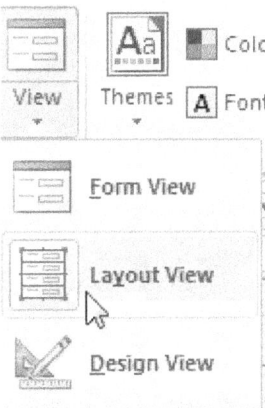

Now the first thing you might want to do in Layout mode here is to resize some of the objects on your Form, for example you can see that FirstName and LastName have pretty big Textboxes. I don't need them to be that large so lets make them shorter. I'll move my mouse over the border there, notice how it changes into a double pointing arrow, at this point just click and drag and you'll notice that the entire row gets resized, notice that FirstName and Phone number over here on right also got resized. When you're in Layout mode Access tends a work in columns and rows.

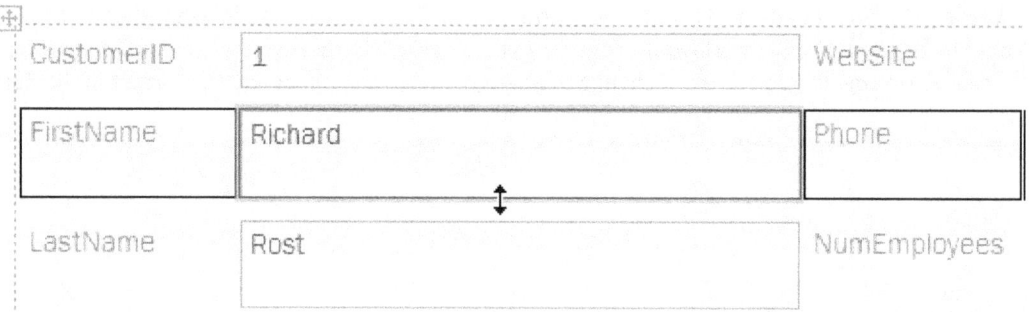

So if you want to resize the column for example just move right here, on the right border of one of the Textboxes and in the column click and drag and notice how the entire column is changed.

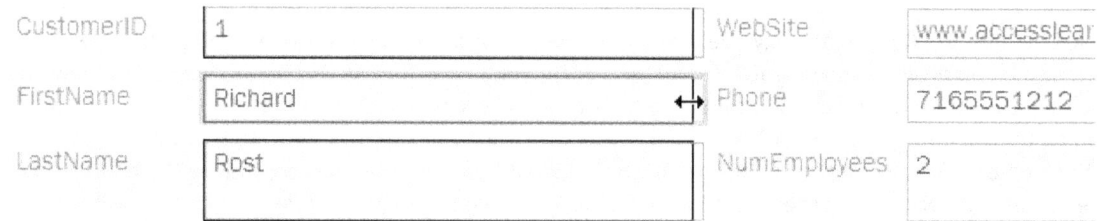

You could also do that with the Labels themselves, click over here on `FirstName` and you can change the width of that column, so take a few minutes now and practice resizing these Textboxes to be the height and width that you want.

And there we go, I'm now happy with the way my Form looks and I'm ready to Save it.

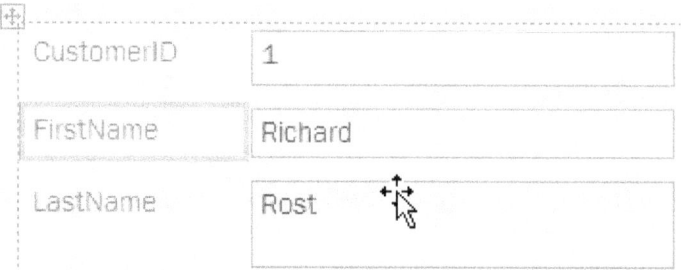

I'm going to come up to the top here and click on the Save button or hit **Ctrl+S**. The SaveAs dialog box appears, I'm going to change this to `CustomerF`, F for Form, remember T for Table, Q for Query, F for Form, R for Report and then I'll hit OK.

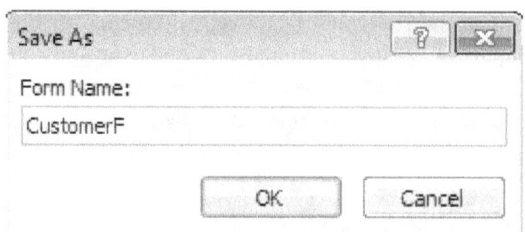

Access 2010 Beginner 1

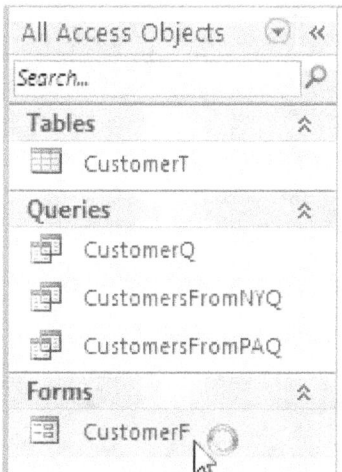

Notice my `CustomerF` is now saved over here in a Forms section in the *Navigation Pane* and it also says `CustomerF` up here on the tab, this still says `CustomerT`, this right here is just a Title for the Form, you can keep this, you can change it or you get rid of it completely, whatever you'd like to do. Personally I never use these so I'm going to click on it and press Delete on my keyboard, that will get rid of it, you can also change or delete this little logo right here, I'm going to get rid of it, that'll save me some space on the screen, I almost never use those little Titles and Logos up top on the Form.

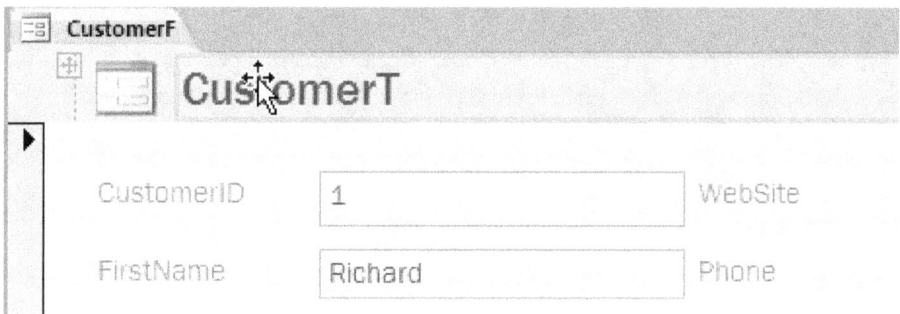

If you want to edit or change them or make new ones you'll find them on the *Design* tab right over here were it says Logo, Title and you can also add a Date and Time, again well take about these in more detail in the next class.

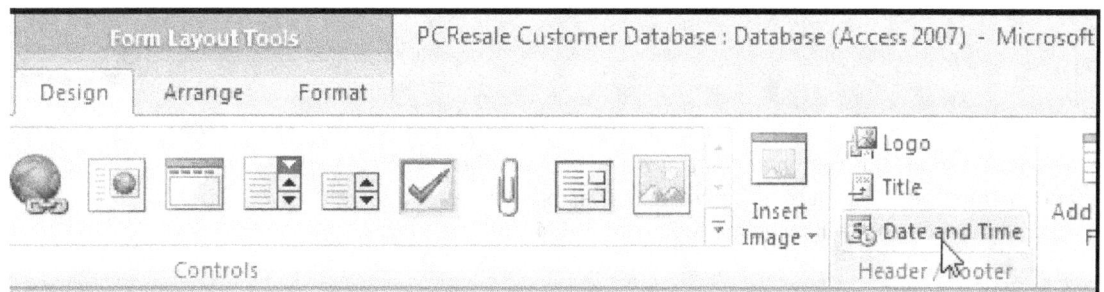

Now that my Form is finished I'm going to come over here and click on the close button, Access asks me if I want to Save the changes to the design of the Form because I deleted that Title and Logo, I'll say Yes. The Form is closed and now I can open it back up by double-clicking on the Customer Form over here, now I'm in Form View.

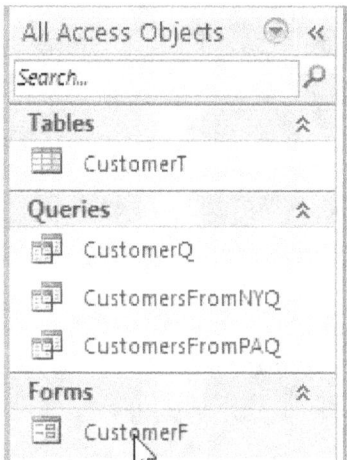

Form View is where your users will work all the time. This is where you come in and make changes to the data in the Form, remember this data is not actually saved in the Form it's really saved in the Table, the Form is just displaying it for you in a different way, so any change you make here in are reflected in the data in your Table.

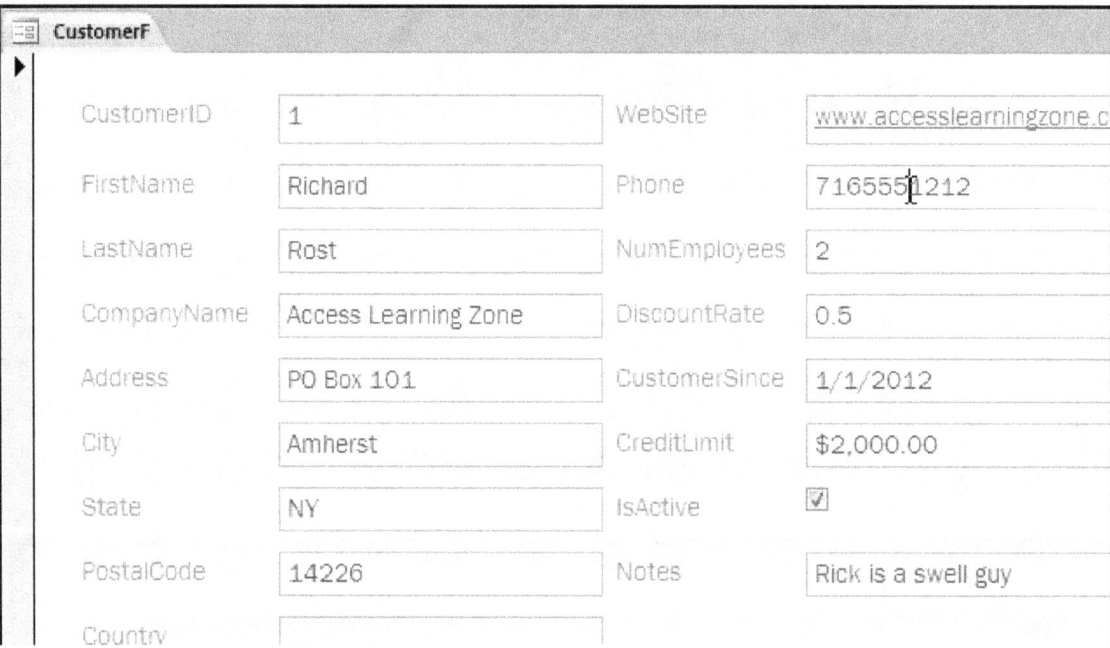

Let's say for example this customer changes his Phone number, I can come right in here and type in the new phone number. If I want to move between the Records I can come right down here and click on these *Navigation* buttons, that will move me to Record 2, 3, 4 and backwards.

This ◄ button moves me to the first Record, this ►► button moves to the last Record.

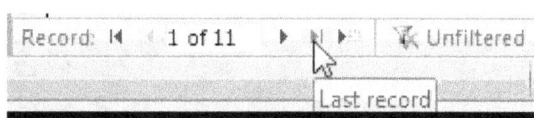

And this little button moves me to a new blank Record so you can begin entering a new Customer.

So I can click on the `FirstName` Field and start typing in a new Customer: New Guy, XYZ Corp. I'm using the tab key to move from Field to Field, remember the pencil over here indicates this is a dirty record, it hasn't been saved to the Table yet, it will be saved as soon as I move off of this Record or close the Form.

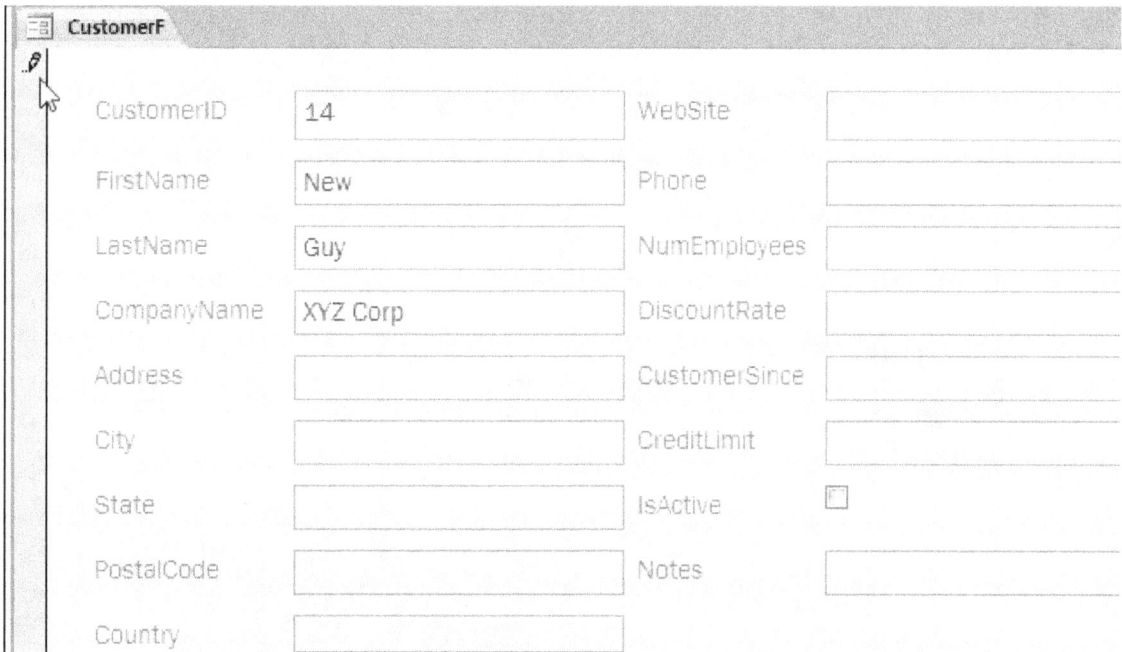

If you wish to delete a Record, simply click anywhere on this big tall bar over here on the left side of the Form, that's called the *Record Selector*, once you click on that you can press the Delete key on your keyboard to delete this record. Access will warn you, "You are about to delete 1 record(s), Are you sure?". If you say Yes you cannot undo that, the Record will be gone for good.

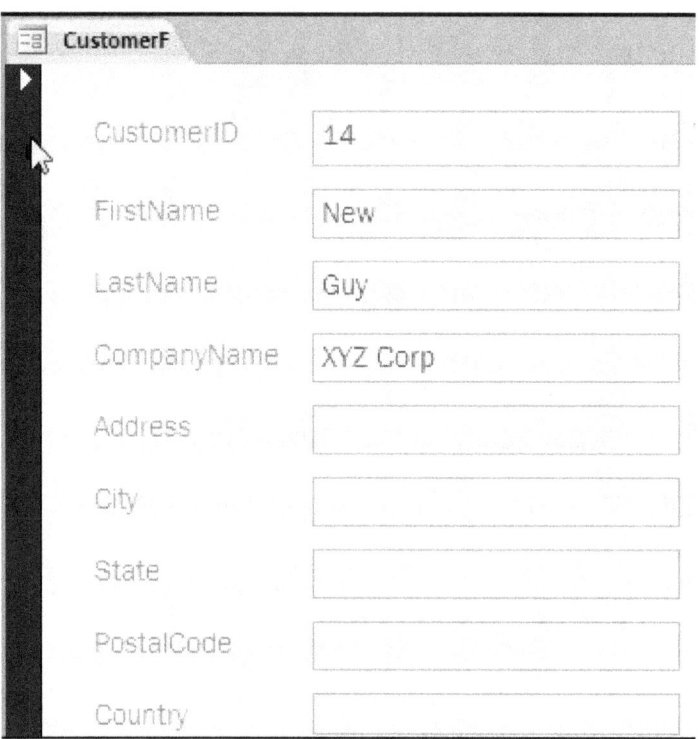

You will also find buttons on the *Ribbon* to Sort and Filter, work with Records such as Delete, Save, Go to a New Record and so on. There are also Find and Replace buttons, we'll talk about all these features in much more detail in the next class.

For now let's just close this Form by clicking over here. I want to quickly show you how to create two additional types of Forms that are extremely handy so click on `CustomerT` then click on *Create*, come over here to More Forms and then you'll see Multiple Items, and click on Multiple Items.

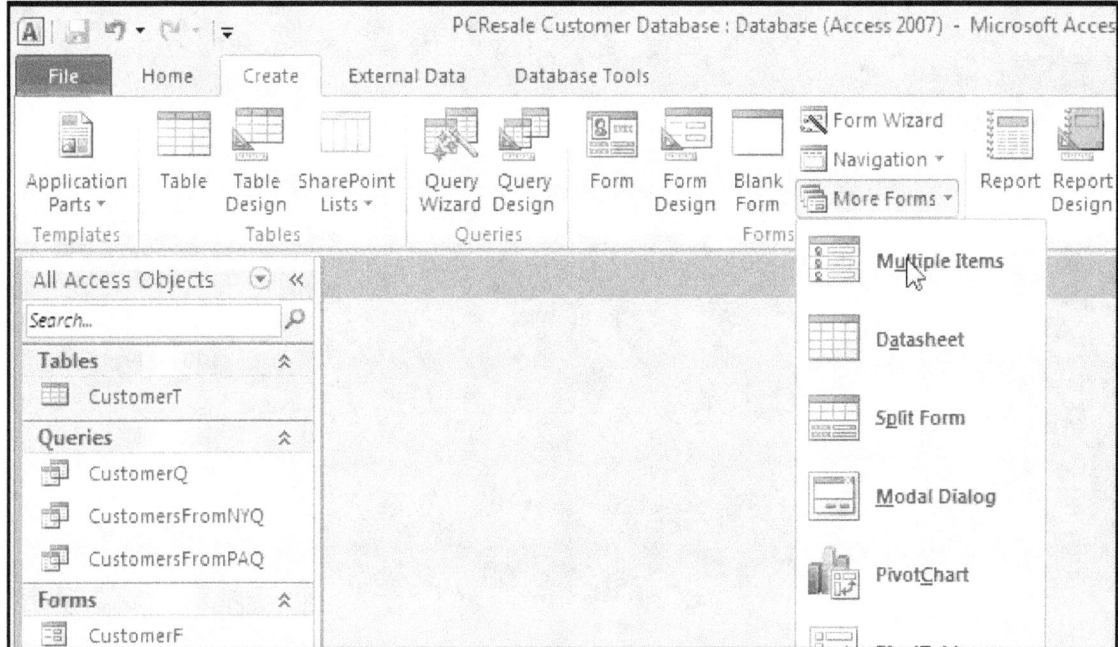

Again Access throws together a quick Form for you but notice how on the screen you can see multiple Records. I'm in Layout Mode so I'm going to resize this because it made the rows very tall but notice here you can see all the different Customers on one Form. This is called a Continuous Form, we will spend a lot more time with this type of Form in future classes but I know a lot of people always ask me how to create these so I wanted to show you where it is real quick.

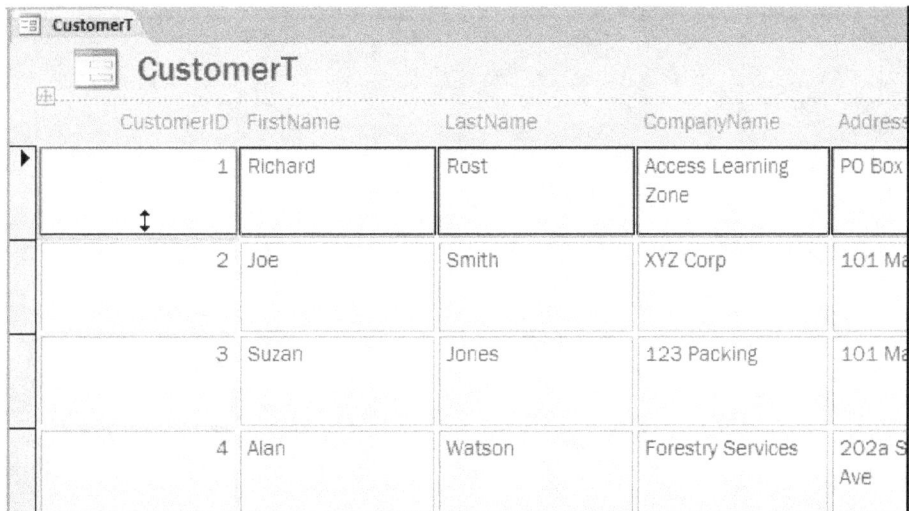

Another very handy type of Form, click on *Create*, More Forms and there's one here called the Split Form.

Access 2010 Beginner 1   Page 73 of 94

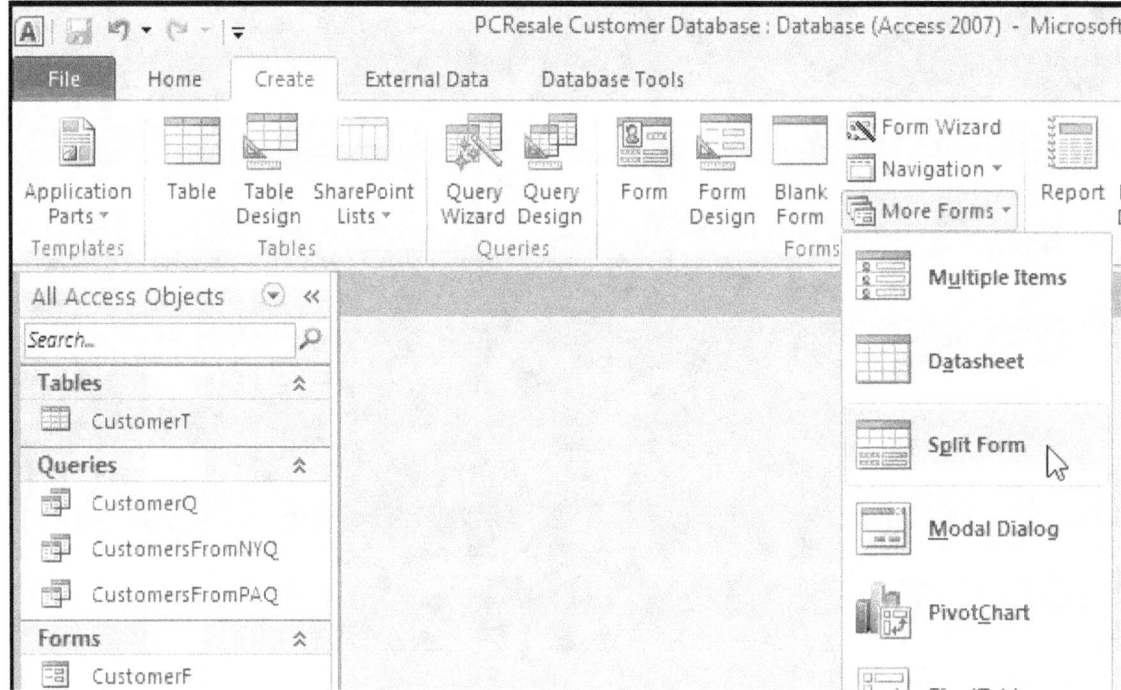

The Split Form is a combination of a standard single Form up top and a Datasheet View on the bottom and as you click between the different Records on the bottom you can see it moves the current Record on the top and again this is very handy, you can scroll down to your list of Customers, click on the one you want to see and that Customer's information is loaded in the top half of the Form, again that's called a Split Form.

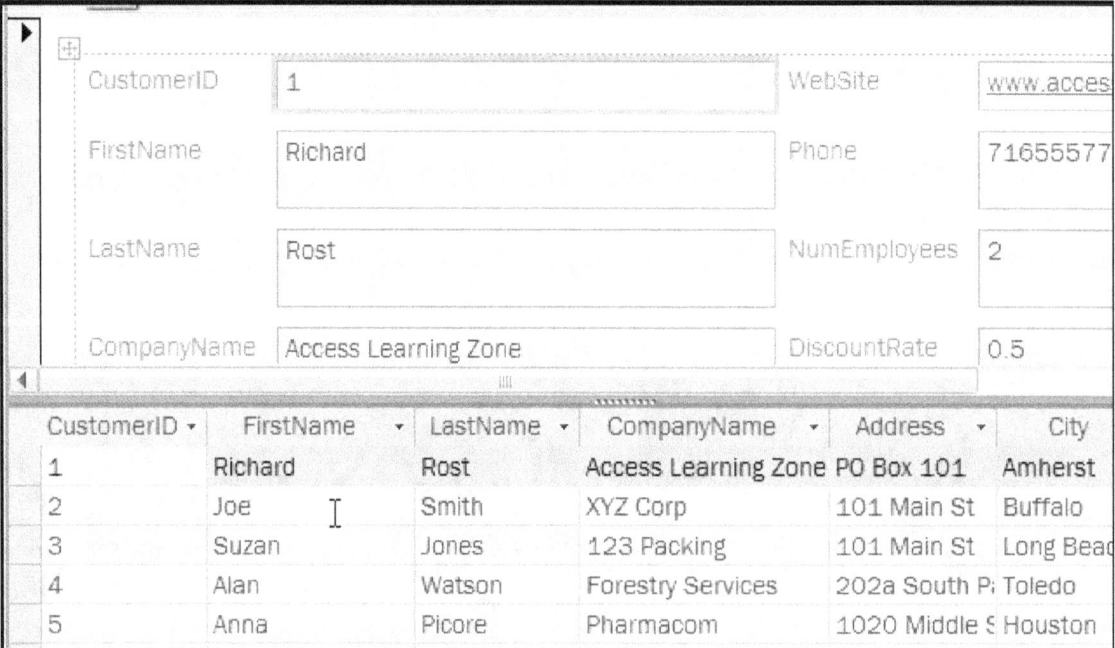

These are just a couple of examples of the many different types of Forms that you can build in Access and again over the next couple of classes I will show you how to create lots and lots of different types of

Forms. For now, again, I'm going to close this Form and I'll say No to Save changes, so that in a nutshell is how you can build a simple Customer Form.

Lesson 11: Customer Reports

In Lesson 11 we'll build a couple of Customer Reports including a few Customer Mailing labels.

So far we've learned how to create Tables, Queries and Forms. Reports are pretty much just like Forms and are designed to be printed out or sent as an e-mail attachment or basically presented to someone who's not using your database.

Creating a Report is very similar to creating a Form, first to click on the Table or Query that has our data in, then we click on *Create* and over to the right we'll see the Reports section. It's very similar to the Forms section.

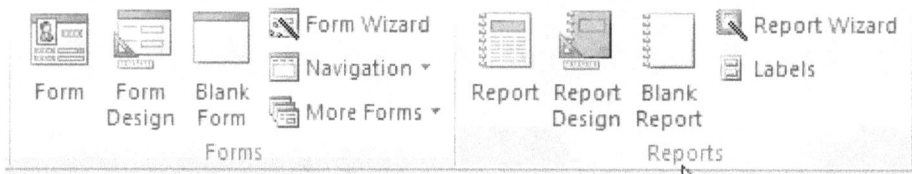

First we have the basic Report where Access just builds us a Report.

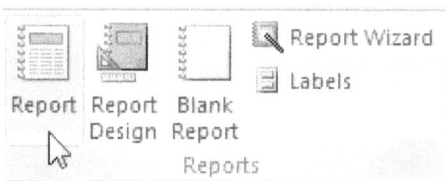

Report Design, that lets us get in and modify the nooks and crannies of the Report, we'll talk about Report Design in a future class.

We have the Blank Report where Access just throws a Blank Report together and lets you insert Fields where you want them.

We have a Report Wizard which will ask you some questions and design the Report that way.

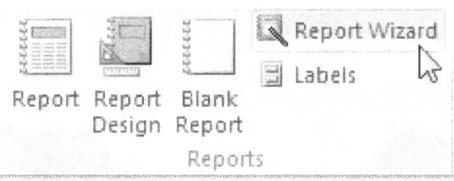

And finally there's a Labels Wizard right here which is used for creating Mailing Labels. We will walk through the Labels Wizard a few minutes.

But first let me show you the basic Report. I'm just going to click on the Report button and after a moment Access throws this Report together for us. As you can see Access put together a simple Customer Report. It looks just like a Continuous Form that we built earlier in our Forms section. If I scroll down I'll see multiple Customers, one per line, if I go back up to the top of the Report, you can see there is a Report header up here, you can again delete that Title if you want to, you can double-click on it and type something in like Customer Report and then press Enter.

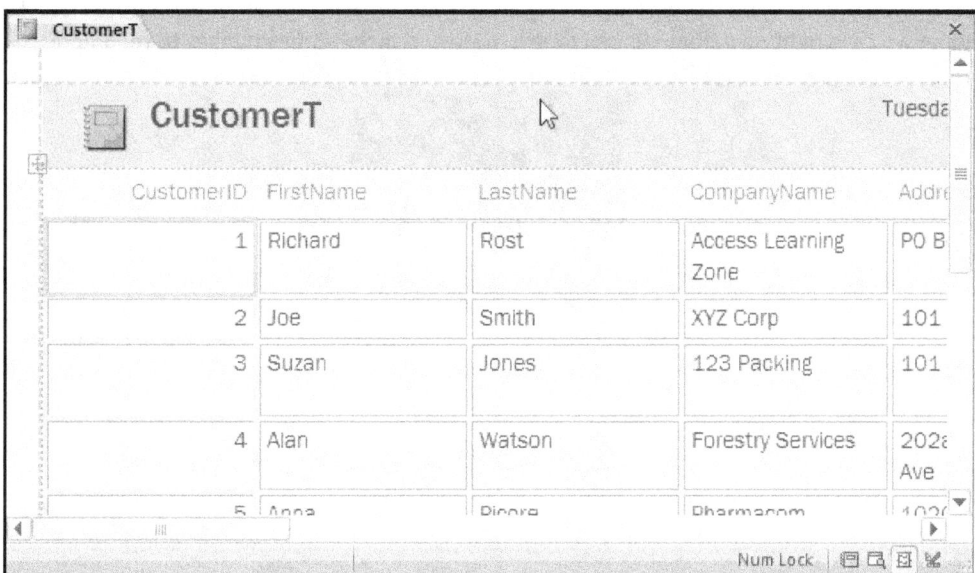

Notice over on the right you'll see the Time and Date, this is usually handy on reports so you can see when the Report was printed.

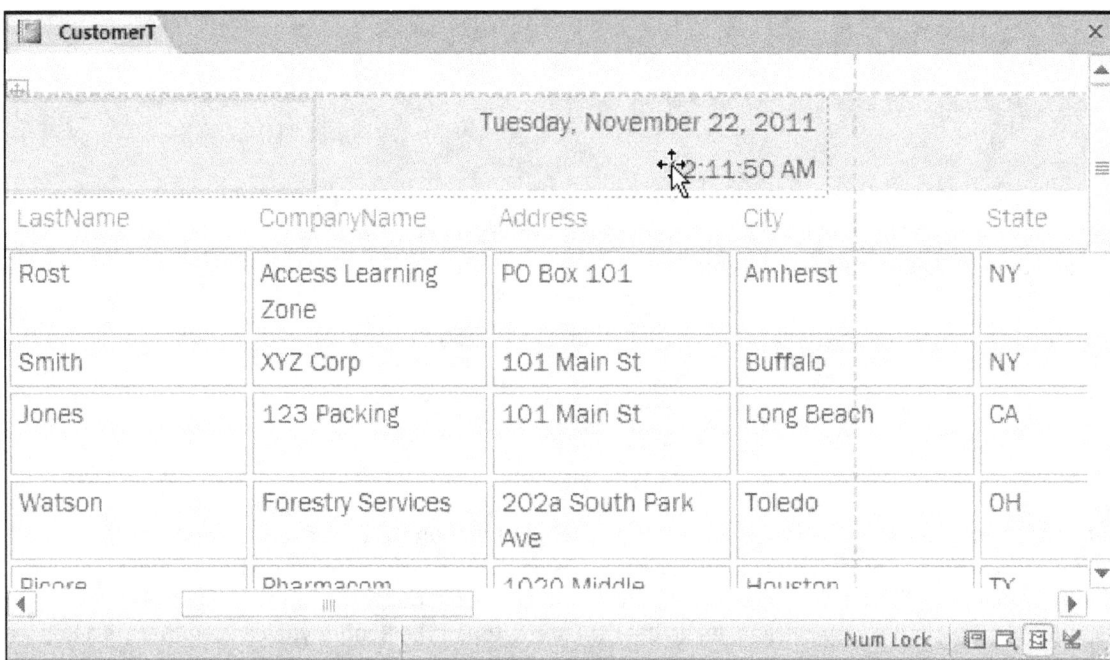

Again just like Forms, Reports have different views. There is Report View; Print Preview; Layout View, which we are in right now; and Design View, now Design View we will talk about in a future class, Layout View is what we're in right now, that lets us come in here and make some changes to the Report.

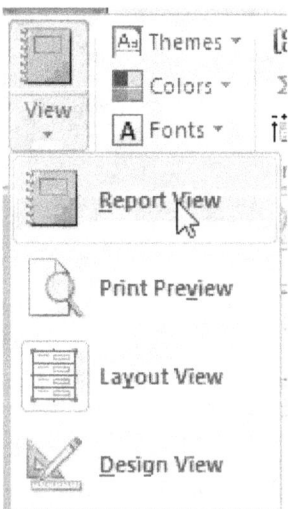

Now you have a limited control over the height of these objects because Access needs to print all of the information in each text box so as you can see here the CompanyName is forced onto a second line so it has to be able to grow that Textbox vertically in order to show the information, you can get away without doing this on Forms because on a Form a Textbox you can scroll up and down, you can't quite do that on Report, so the Report you could really only easily control the horizontal size.

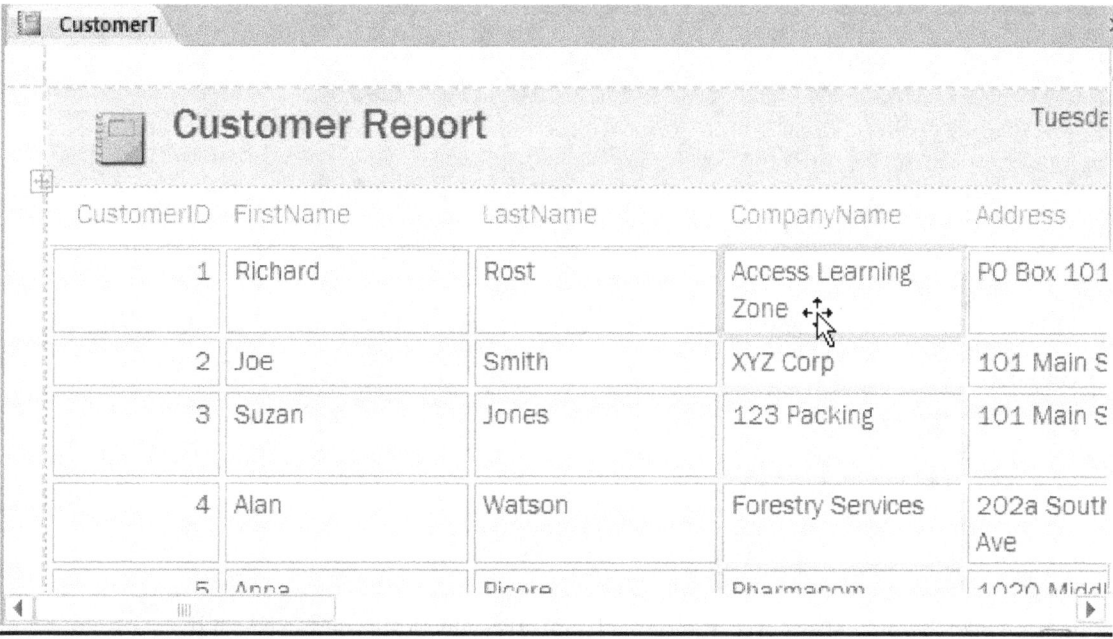

If you want to see where this is going to look like when you actually print it, come over here and go to Print Preview.

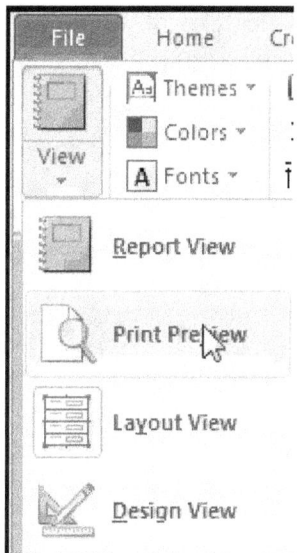

This will give you a better approximation of what your Report is going to look like when it's printed. Notice in the bottom here we have zoom controls just like in Word and Excel where we can zoom out to get a better view of a document, we can scroll down, we can go to Page 2 right here, then Page 3.

You can change the size of the page, Letter; Legal; Executive and so on, you can adjust the margins right here. Right now they are set to narrow, you can set to Wide or Normal.

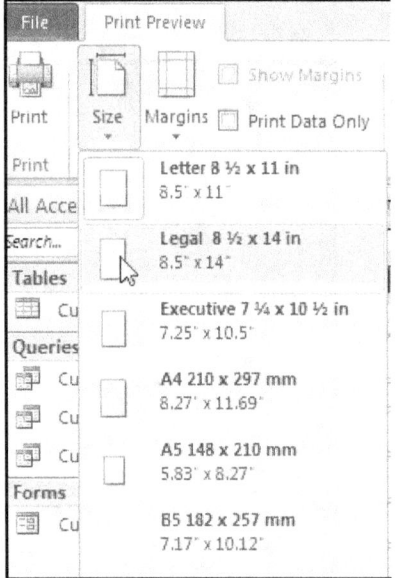

Here is we could also come to Export this Report as a data file. If you want to send it as an E-mail Attachment click on E-mail. You can Export it as a PDF file or send it to a text file or even Excel file. I'll click on the PDF or XPS button.

Browse to where you want to save the File, change the File name if you want to and then SaveAs type I'll leave as PDF, then I'll come over here and click on Publish.

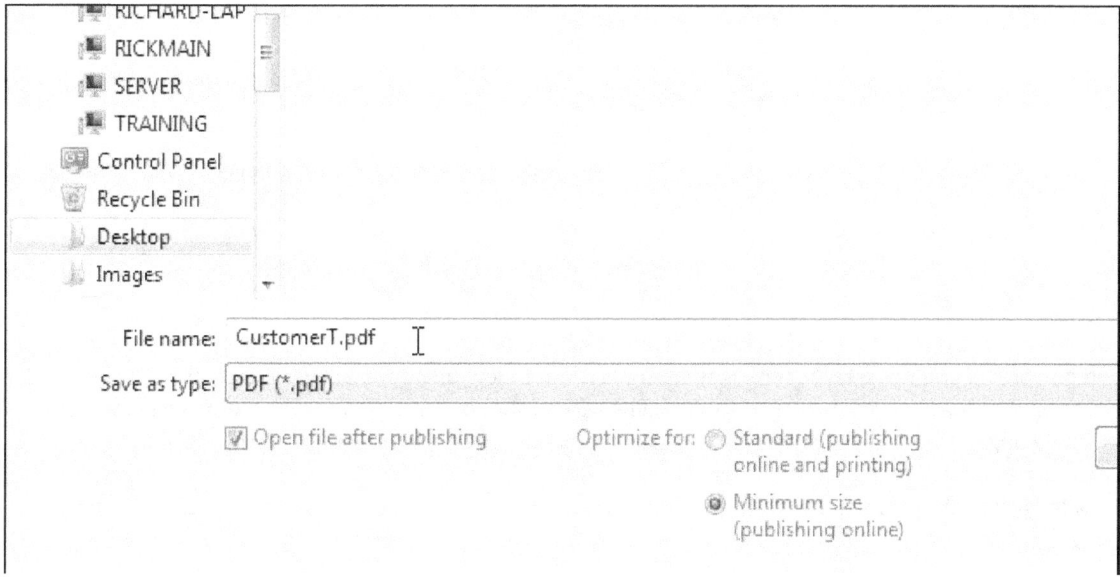

And now I have a nice formatted PDF file that I can save for later, e-mail someone, put my website.

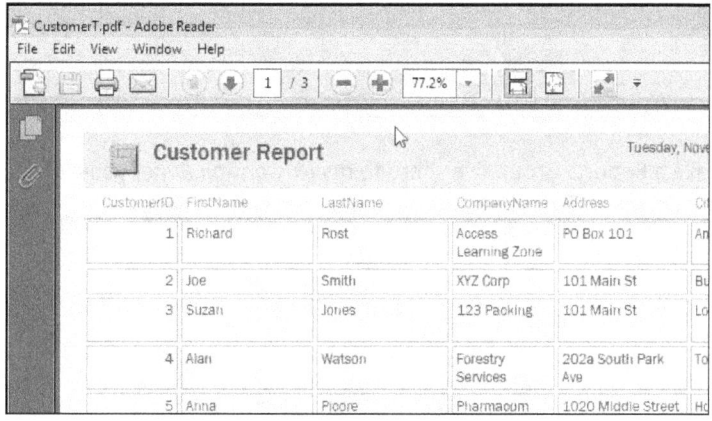

I'll go ahead and close that.
Access is asking us if what save these Export steps for the future, I'm just going to close this, we'll talk about this later, essentially if you have certain reports that you Export on a regular basis you can save the steps so you don't have to repeat the Wizard everytime. We'll talk more about this in a future class.

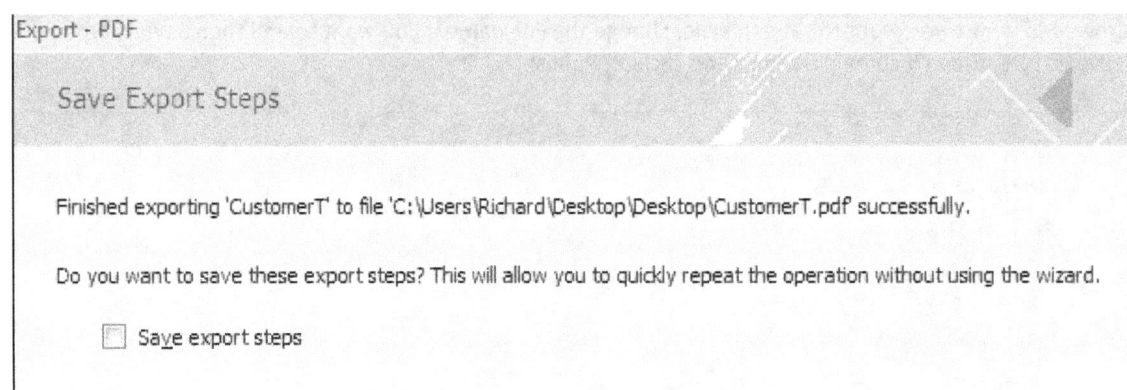

There is not a ton of difference between Layout View and Report View. Report View shows you the data and doesn't let you make layout changes whereas Layout View obviously allows you to make those changes. When you have your end users opening up your Reports you don't want them playing with the layout changes and yes in a future lesson I'll show you how to restrict all that.

Now let's close this Report. Do I want to save this Report? Sure I'll Save this as my `CustomerR` and then hit OK.

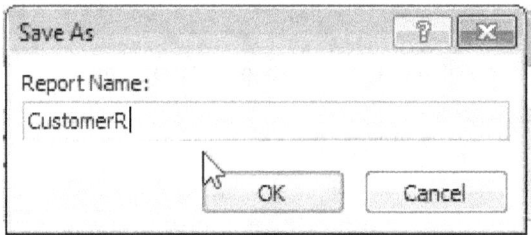

Now you can see I have a Reports Group over here to my *Navigation Pane*, you can see `CustomerR` is right there. To open it up again I'll double-click on it and then close it again.

Now sometimes you might want to make a Report based on data from a Query, for example let's see the boss only want to see those customers from New York again, this time click on CustomersFromNYQ, Go to *Create*, click on Report.

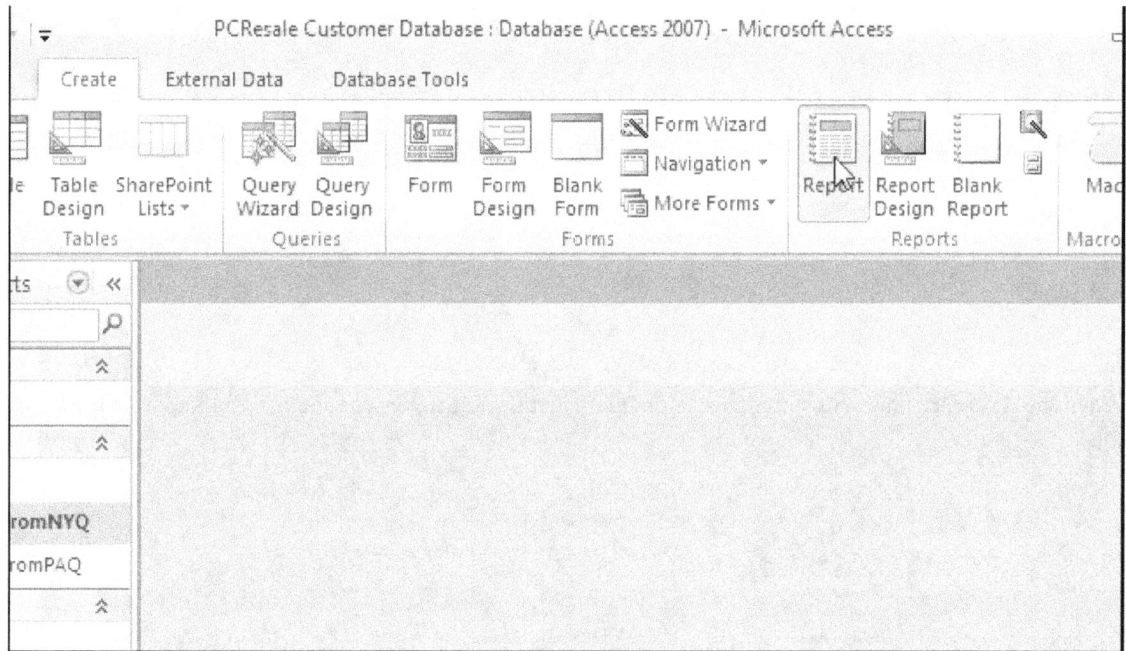

Now the Report is only getting its data from the Query so as you can see here I'm only getting 5 records instead of all 11 and I can change this Report header by just clicking in it and editing it that way: CustomersFromNY.

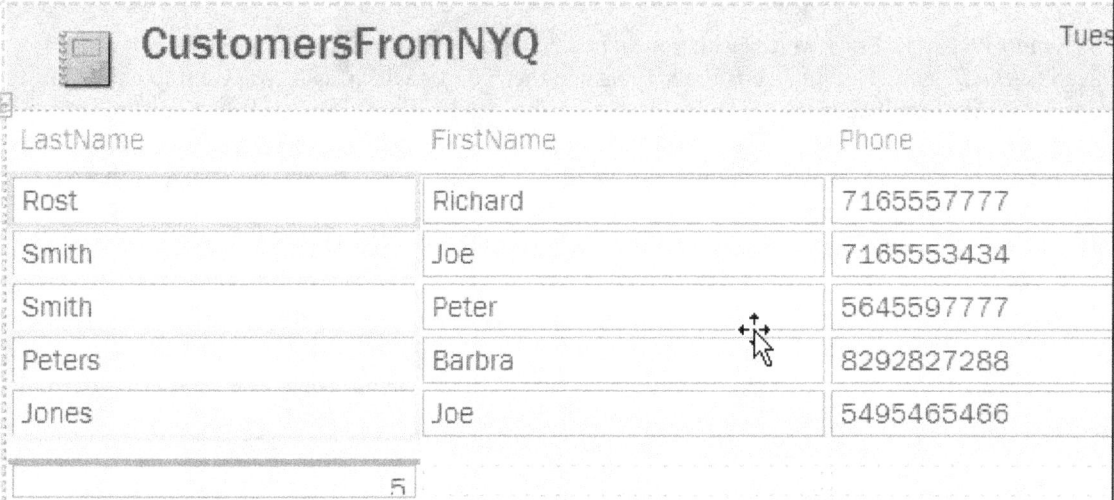

If you want a Report that looks more like this, the single Form, where you only have one Customer per page:

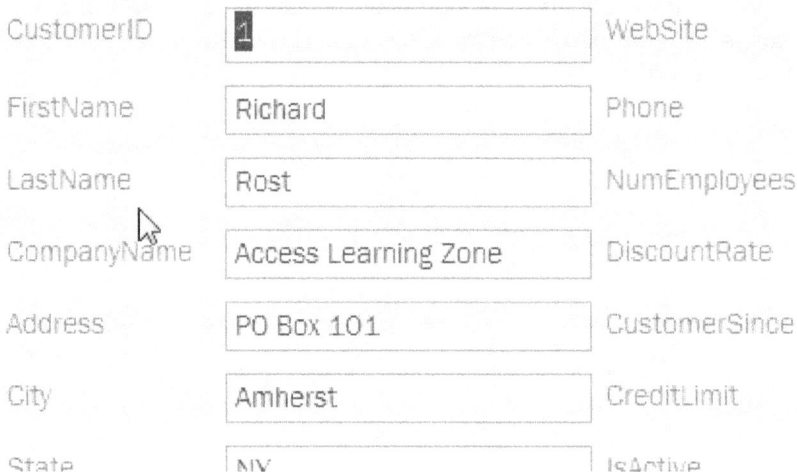

What you do is click on the Customer Table or Query if you want to, *Create* and use the Report Wizard for this.

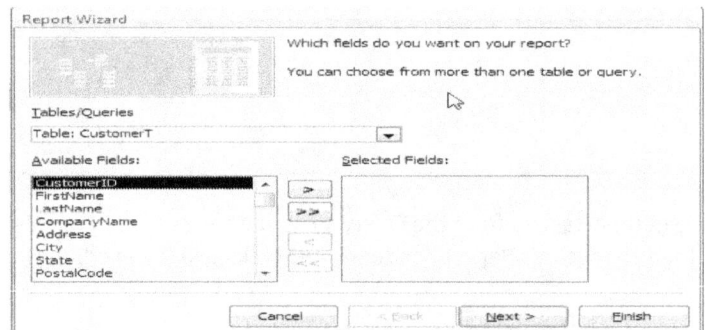

The Report Wizard first says which Fields you want any Report. Pick the Table or Query here, if you haven't already, we'll stick with a Customer Table and then choose which Fields you want to be on this Report. Lets say I don't need the `CustomerID`, how about the `FirstName`, click on it and then click on this arrow here, that moves it from the available Fields or the selected Fields and `LastName` you could also just double-click on the field like this, how about `City`, `State` and `Phone` number, just those Fields. I'll click Next.

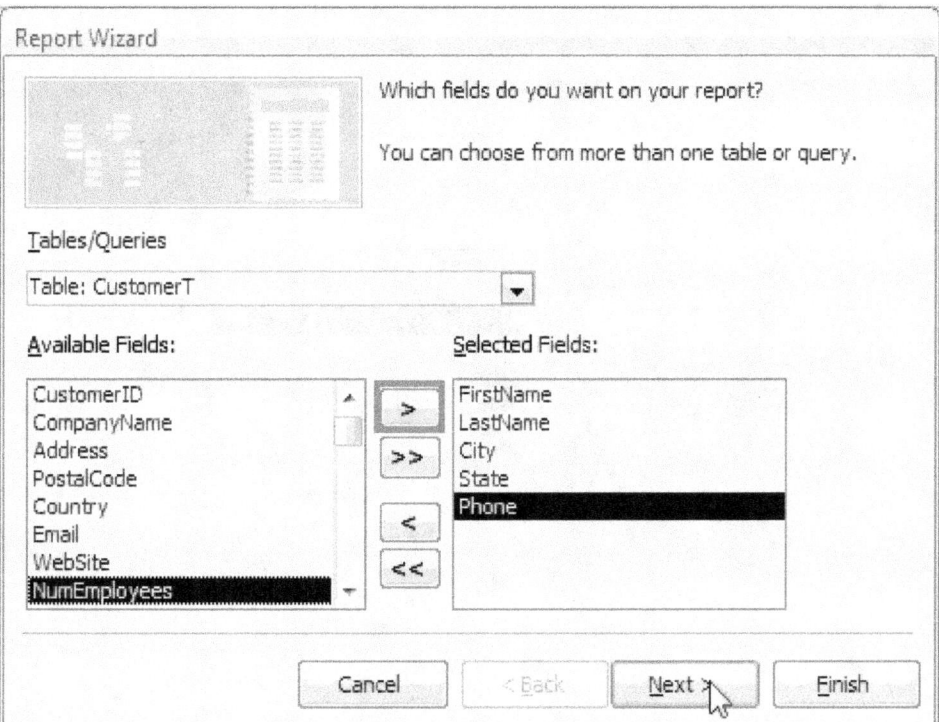

Do you to want to add any Grouping levels. This is handy if you want to Group all of the Customers from New York together for example, but for now I just skip this and click Next.

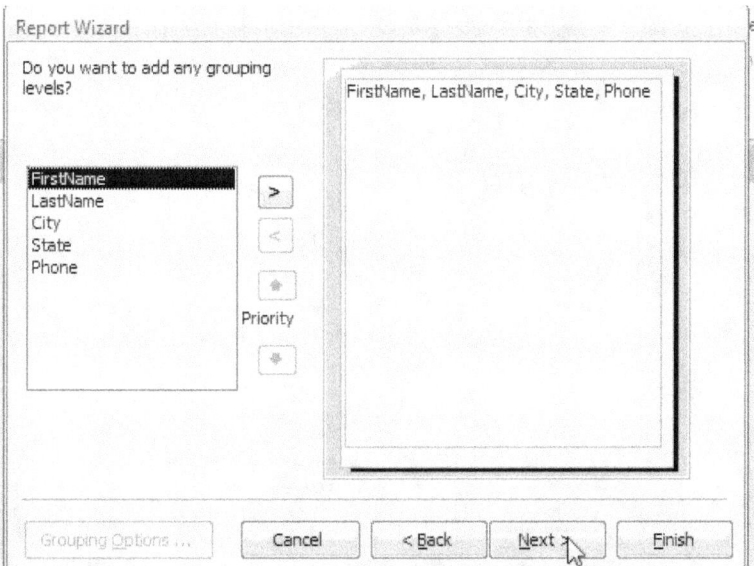

What Sort Order do you want for your Records, lets say you want to sort by `LastName`. You can Sort by up to four different Fields, Next.

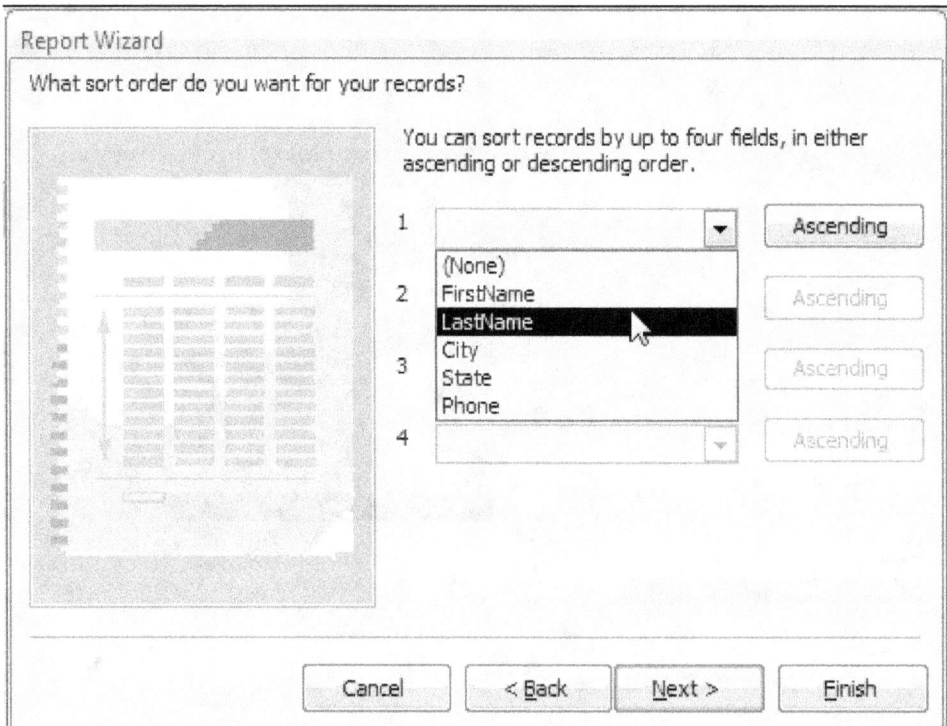

How do you want the Report to look, Tabular is the look we had earlier, theres also Columnar: which is the look were looking for and Justified look, lets go with Columnar and in a corner hit Next.

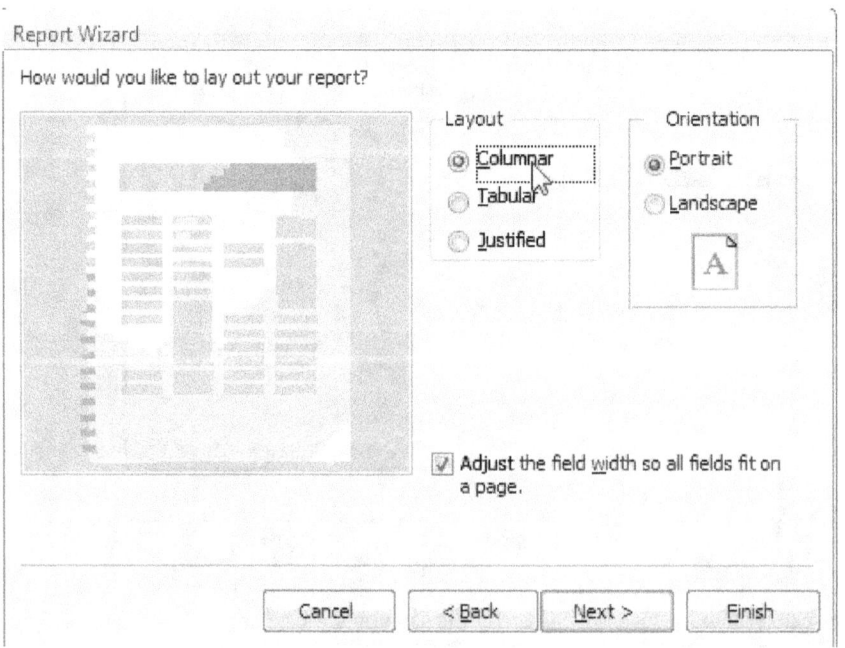

What Title do you want the top of the Report. Lets change this to Customers, that's what goes in the Title box and then Finish.

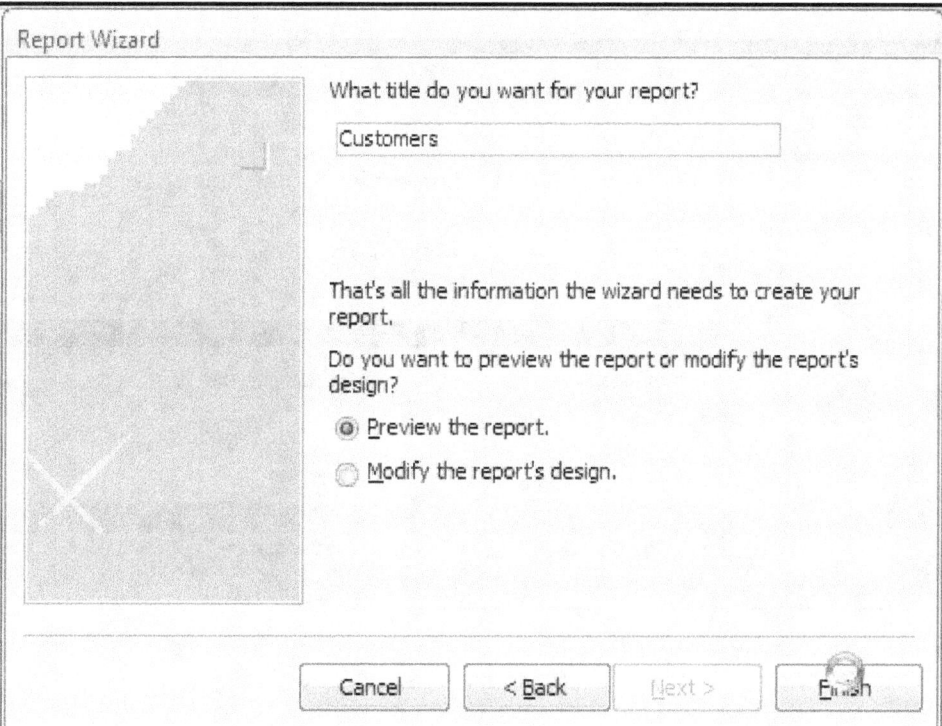

After a second Access puts the Report together for you and puts you in Print Preview mode and there we are. Notice my mouse pointer has changed to a magnifying glass, if you click somewhere on the Report it zooms you out. Click to zoom back in again. Notice you see just the Fields that you requested to be on the report, we picked those in the Wizard.

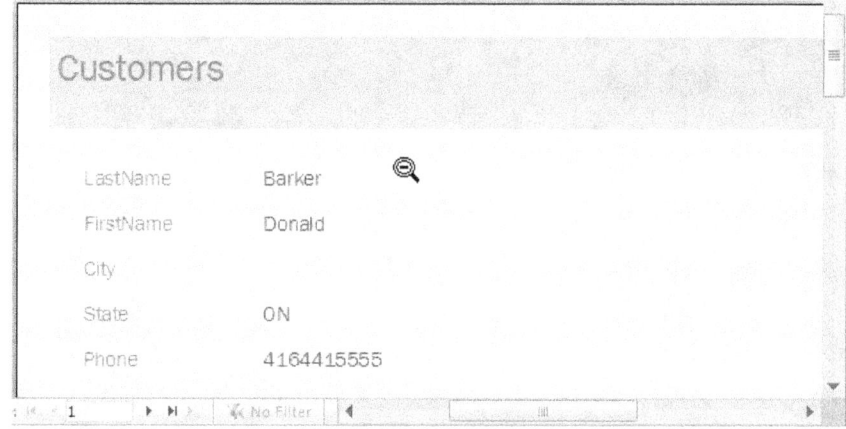

Now let's make some Mailing Labels. Click on CustomerT, hit Create and then in the Reports section click on Labels, the Label Wizard loads up, come down here where it says "Filter by manufacturer" and find the manufacturer of the type of labels that you want to use. There are a ton of different manufacturers and I'm using Avery labels, then find the product number. Each Avery label type has a product number. I'm using 5160s, that's the label that gives you 30 per page, there is 3 across and 10 down. I'll click Next.

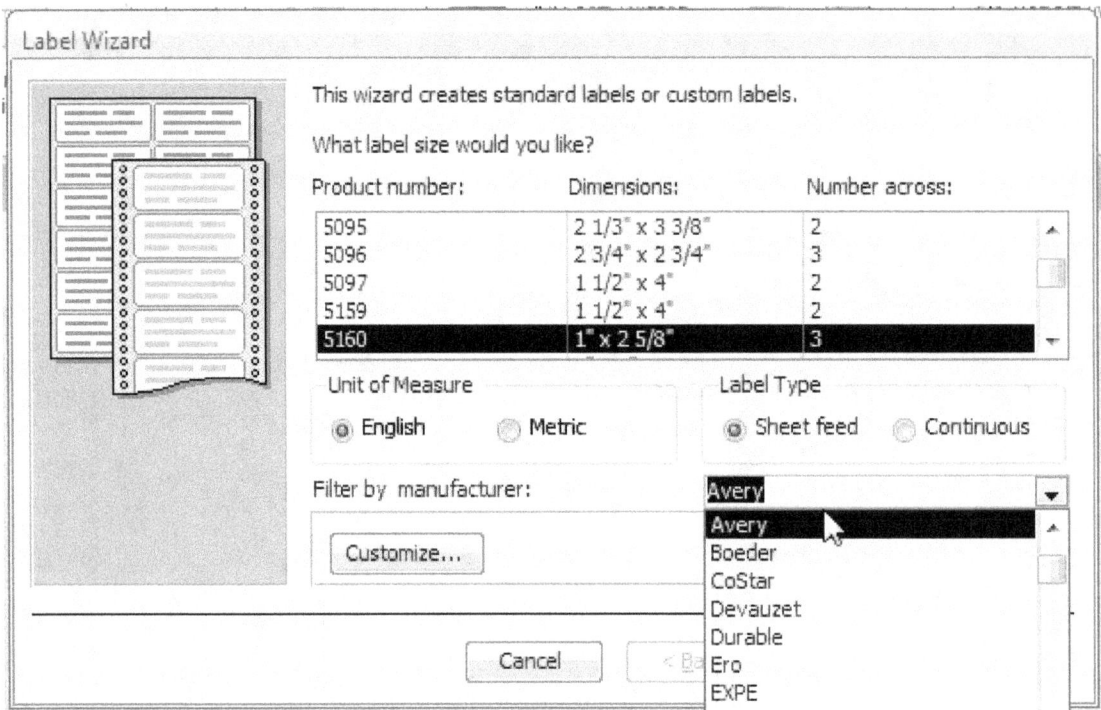

Choose the Font, the Font Size, the Font Weight and the color that you want for the Font on your labels again I'll just press Next.

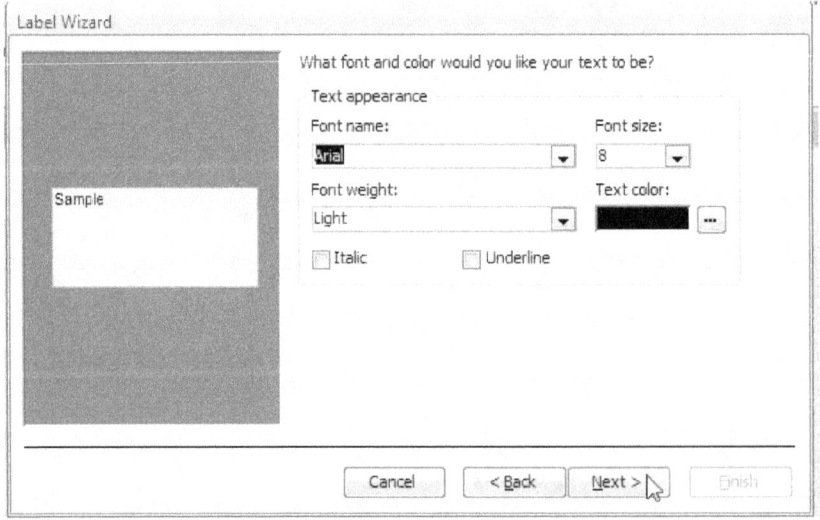

Now we're asked to set up a Protype Label. Essentially this is what you want your mailing labels to all look like. I'll start with `FirstName`, now you can either double-click on it or click on it once and then press this button here. Following `FirstName` I want a space so I'll press Spacebar on my keyboard, then `LastName`. Now to move down to the next line, I'll press Enter. `CompanyName` is next, Enter. `Address`, Enter, and finally `City`, Spacebar, `State`, Spacebar, `PostalCode`, Spacebar, `Country`, that's another reason why I wanted to keep `Country` blank because most of my Customers are from the US so it just won't print anything there, if it's different `Country` like Canada it should show Canada, now press Next.

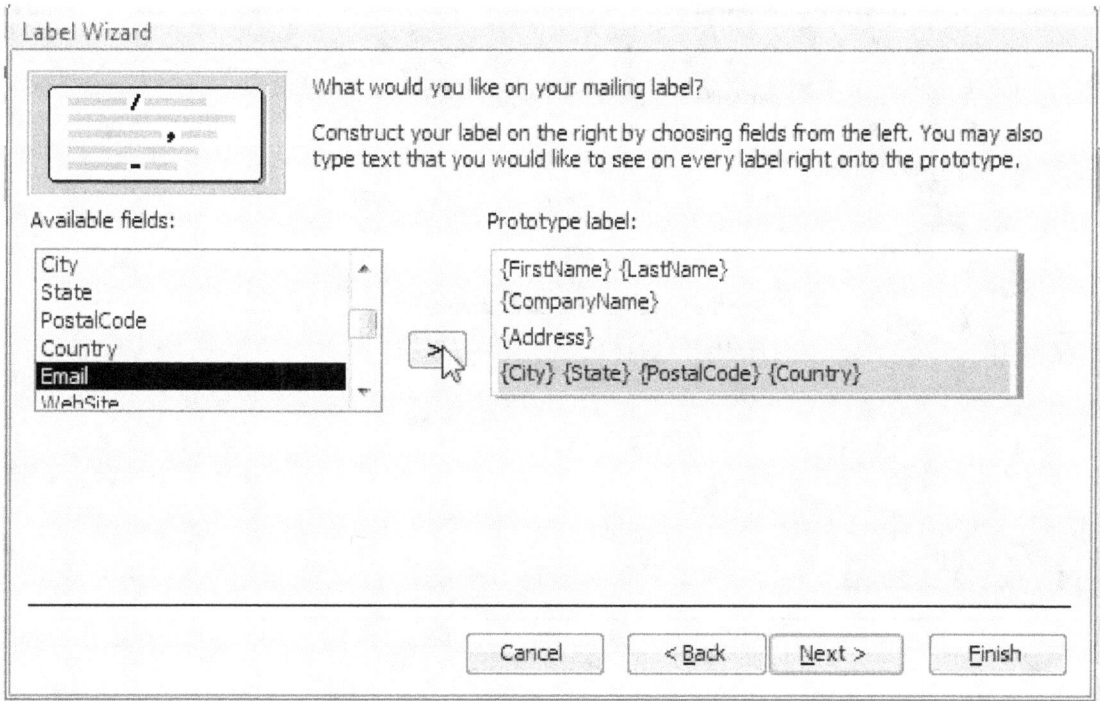

Which Fields would like to Sort By, if you're running bulk mail you might wanna pick `PostalCode`, press Next.

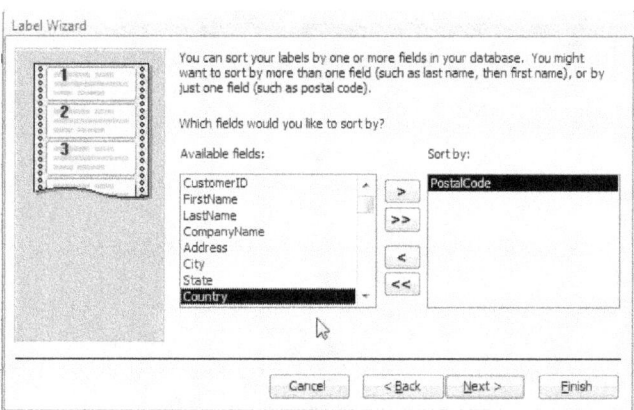

What name would like for the the Report. I will go with `CustomerMailingLabelR`, R for Report, then finally I'll click Finish.

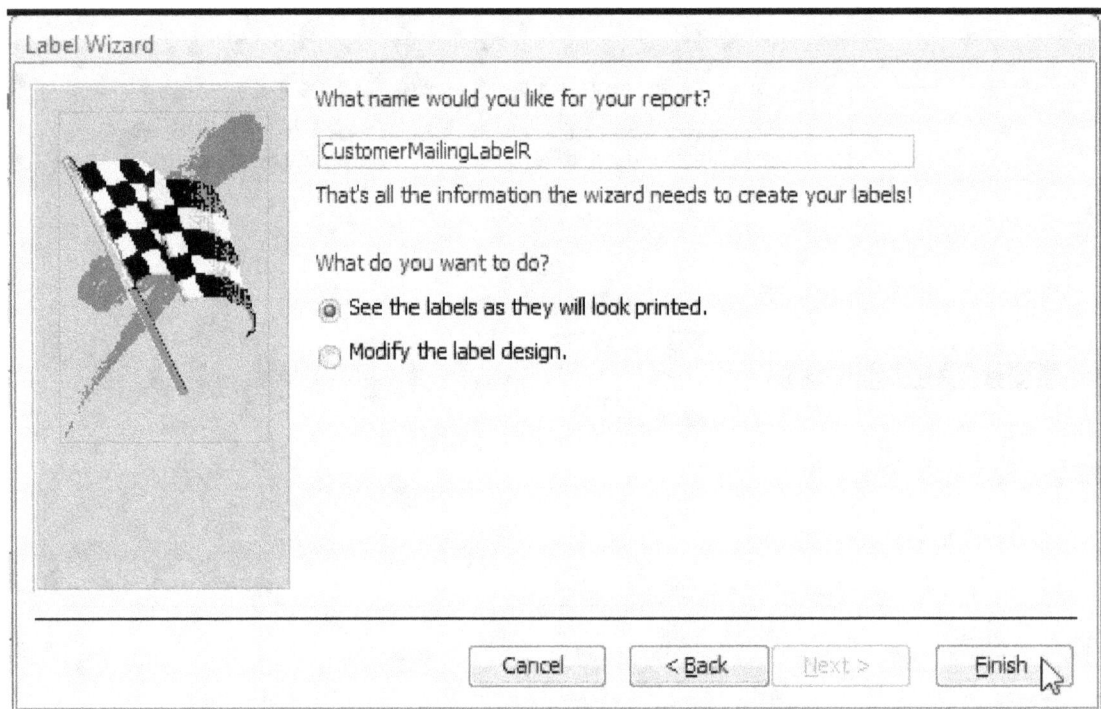

You can see the Print Preview of our Mailing Labels. You can click and zoom out and see all the Mailing Labels. Now you just had to feed this into your printer and click on the Print button.

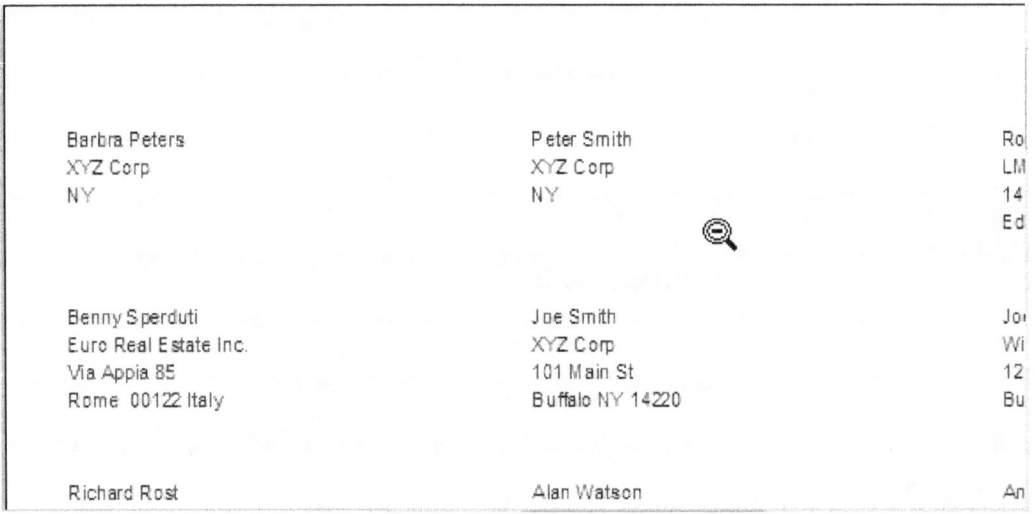

The Print button is right here on the left hand side of the Print Preview tab.

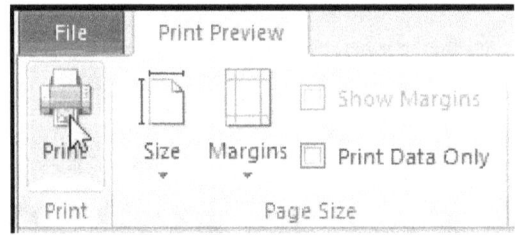

When you're done just click the close Print Preview button, this will actually put you into Design Mode. Notice in Design Mode you can see the different individual Textboxes, you can and Details section, the Page Header bars up here, we will talk about all these things in the future classes, for now I'll just close the Report.

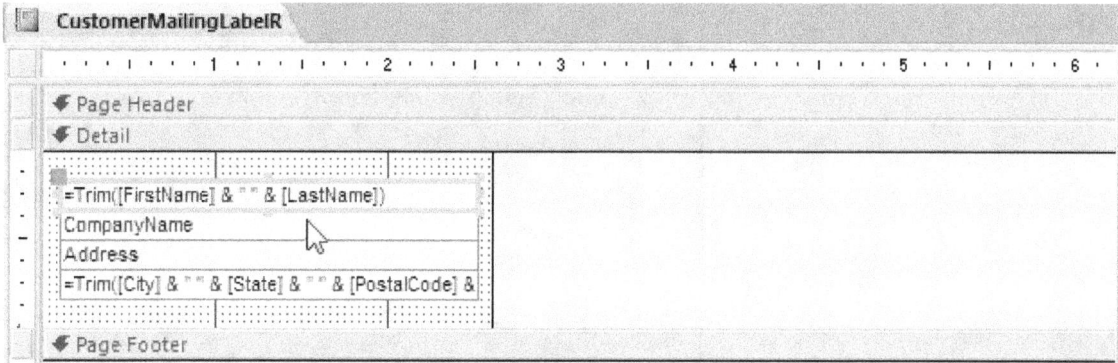

Now if you go to run this Report in the future, if you double click on it, it will open up the Report in Report View and you'll see here that you don't have any columns.

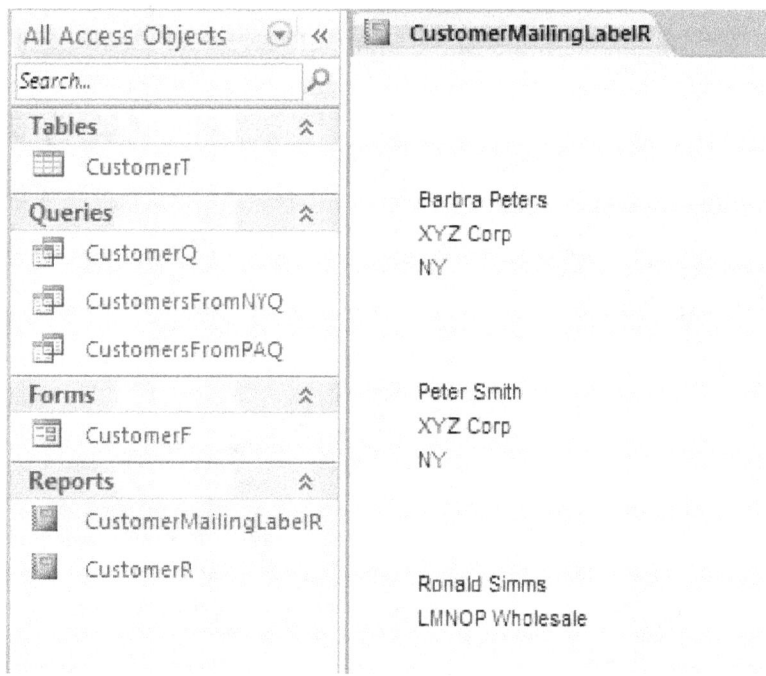

In order to see your columns you'll have to come up here and drop this down and go to Print Preview.

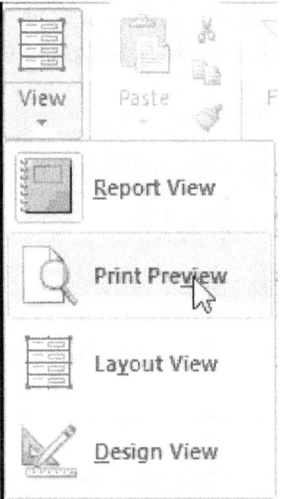

Some of you might also get this warning message, it says "Some data may not be displayed there is not enough horizontal space in the page for the number of columns in the column spacing you specified." Essentially the columns and the column spacing need to be adjusted, usually this is because of the print drivers you have in your system, we will talk about different remedies for this in the future lessons but for now just click OK and your Report should still be displayed.

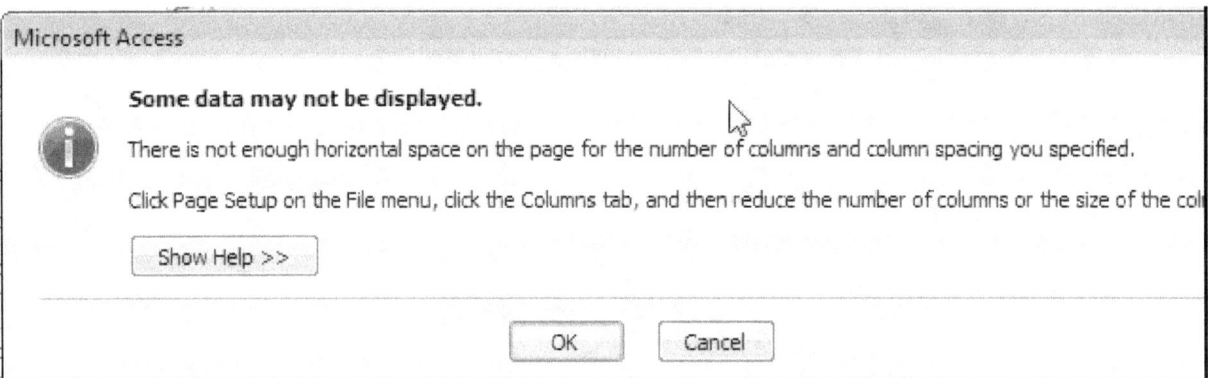

In a future lesson I'll teach you how to deal with that error message and show you how to make a button on your Navigation Form and we will make a Main Menu that will open up this Report or even print it directly without having to switch in the Print Preview mode. For now let's just close this Report.

So now we've built a Customer Table, a couple of different Customer Queries, a Customer Form, a simple Customer Report and some Customer Mailing Labels. You now have the beginnings of a great Access database that you're building yourself. Over the next couple classes we'll add lots more to this database and you'll see everything that Access can do.

Review

Let's take a moment now to review what we covered in class.

- Database terminology
- Planning your database
- The Access Interface
- Building a Customer Table
- Entering & Editing Data
- Sorting & Filtering
- Customer Queries
- Constructing a Customer Form
- Customer Reports & Labels

Sample Code

- 599CD.com/XACDATA1

Links

- AccessLearningZone.com
- AccessLearningZone.com/contact
- AccessLearningZone.com/forums
- AccessLearningZone.com/databases

> **RICK'S NOTE:**
> I really do enjoy getting surveys from you! Make sure you visit the web page above and fill out the survey for this class. Let me know if I've moved too fast, and whether or not I covered material that was helpful to you!
> http://www.AccessLearningZone.com/survey

What's next?
Microsoft Access 2010 Beginner Level 2

Contact Us.
If you have any questions, visit www.AccessLearningZone.com/contact or post your question(s) on the Student Forum discussion board.

Credits:
Course development: Richard Rost
Handbook authoring: Richard Rost III
Editing & additional authoring: Alex Hedley

Copyright Notice / Terms of Use

This course, handbook, videos, and other materials are © **COPYRIGHT** 2012 by Amicron Computing. All rights reserved. No portion of this course, handbook, videos, or other course materials may be reproduced, copied, edited, or otherwise distributed without the express written permission of Amicron Computing. Amicron Computing shall not be held liable for any errors or omissions in this document.

Subject to our **TERMS OF SALE**, Amicron grants you a license for **ONE PERSON** to use this handbook along with the accompanying video tutorial. You may **NOT** transfer your license to use (give or sell) the materials to any other party or person. Your license is non-transferable. This handbook and accompanying video tutorial are sold on a **PER-USER** basis. Your copy is for **YOU** alone. You may not give or sell it to someone else when you're finished with it. We do have volume discounts available for organizations that wish to train multiple people.

This handbook and/or the accompanying video tutorials may **NOT** be used as part of a training course without express, written permission from Amicron Computing and the purchase of an **Instructional License**.

For details, contact:

Amicron Computing
137 Huntleigh Circle
Amherst NY 14226 USA
www.amicron.com
267-295-6093 voicemail
866-603-0320 fax

www.ingramcontent.com/pod-product-compliance
Lightning Source LLC
Chambersburg PA
CBHW080944170526
45158CB00008B/2369